Acknowledgements

The books and periodicals listed be   g
                          his res

George Ferrier : North Berwick

Walter M Ferrier : The North Berwick Story 1980

Gullane and Dirleton History Society : The Stones of Dirleton Churchyard and their People 2007

Bruce Jamieson : Old North Berwick 2000

Ben Millar : Tales of Old North Berwick 1998

Dr James S Richardson : Guide to North Berwick 1907

Haddingtonshire Courier

The author would like to thank the following for their assistance during his research without whom this book would never have been possible:-

Stewart Auld, Vanda Baillie, Sandra Baron, Des Bathgate, Violet Bath-gate, Robert Bee, Charlie Bruce, Sheila Bruce, Margaret Burgon, Ina Coventry, Raymond Coventry, Jean Crawford, Tom Danks, George Day, George Denholm, Moira Dunn, Gordon Elliot, Nancy Elliot, Kay Gilbert, Betty Gilford, Glasgow University Archive Services, Agnes Gorrie, John Gray, HBOS plc Group Archives, Jenny Hardie, Jean Himsworth, Alan Hutchison, James Hutchison, Mary Hutchison, Amy Imrie, Betty Inglis, Frances Laing, Marjory Lauder, Lawrie Lumsden, Doris McAllister, Jean McEwan, Oliver McKemmie, Mary MacLaren, Peggy McNicoll, John Masterton, Gladys Miller, Robert Miller, Barbara Montgomery, Frank Nicolson, Bill Nimmo, North Berwick Day Centre, North Berwick Scouts, Kathy Parker, Johnanna Scott, Douglas Seaton, Muriel Shiel, Alistair Stewart, Irene Stewart, Ross Stewart, Sandy Struth, Jim Thorburn, Ella Vlandy, Clarence Walker, Rosey Walker, Alick Watt, Catherine Watt, Sheila Webster, John Wightman, John Wilson, Ross Wilson, James Young and East Lothian Council's Local History Library.

Thanks also to Christine Gollan for all her help and support.

JF

Introduction

North Berwick is a small coastal town in south east Scotland. Its exact origins are unknown. However, it is safe to conclude that a settlement had existed for some period of time before its importance was officially recognised in 1373 when the town was granted a Royal Charter by King Robert II.

The town's first wave of prosperity came in the thirteenth century with the establishment of a ferry to carry pilgrims over the Forth to Earlsferry. The pilgrims, who had travelled from all over Britain, and even as far as the continent, were on route to St Andrews there to worship the remains of Scotland's patron Saint. Up to 10,000 pilgrims a year were travelling through North Berwick, many staying in the hospice, which had been established in the town to serve their needs. The pilgrims would buy locally produced *souvenirs*, samples of which have been found during recent archaeological digs on the Anchor Green. However by the sixteenth century, traffic was on the wane and by 1692 no ferries were registered at North Berwick.

By the early nineteenth century, prosperity was starting to return again to the burgh. Most of the produce coming into and out of the town was via the harbour. Potatoes and wheat from the rich arable East Lothian farms were exported to other parts of the country. Coal was imported from Fife and Newcastle to satisfy the growing demand for both domestic and commercial uses; a coal-fired foundry was established by Robert Bridges in 1828. A substantial number of the townsfolk were employed directly at the harbour with many more working on the ships and boats plying up and down the coast. The glorious herring fishing days in the first half of the nineteenth century brought further prosperity to the town, and with it the creation of even more new jobs, which were eagerly filled by fishing families from Fife and further up the East Lothian coast, many of whose descendants still live in the town.

However, by the middle of the nineteenth century the town's economy was failing. Herring stocks had started to decline, and the arrival of trawlers off the shore did much harm to the fishermen of the town. Business at the harbour was in decline and the livelihood of its residents was in jeopardy. The arrival of the railway in 1850 resulted in the transfer of the coal yards to the station, adding further to the reduction in shipping work.

Fortunately, North Berwick was on the verge of metamorphosing into something different: the Biarritz of the North. By the 1860s North Berwick was a favourite watering hole for those wishing to take the sea air. Situated on the southern shore of the Firth of Forth, and near its mouth, North Berwick was an ideal location for those wishing to indulge in the benefits of clean air and healthy living. This coupled with the new passion for golf amongst the gentry and prosperous middle classes, brought new opportunities of employment and prosperity for the town. Indeed the association of the town with the aristocracy and parliamentarians of the day aided the Burgh's reputation as the place to be seen. Visitors from all walks of life flocked into the town keen to be associated with it ensuring a healthy local economy. During the late Victorian years the town went through a dramatic transformation with the construction of large villas along the east and west bays, built to provide holiday accommodation for the gentry, either by let or through ownership. Houseroom was scarce, even out of season, when masons and artisans employed in the building of those splendid houses required lodgings.

At this time the High Street and Quality Street also saw dramatic change with many of the old pantiled roofed shops demolished to make way for the fashionable tenements. Shop proprietors would line the station platform awaiting the next influx of butlers and servants, who had been dispatched to prepare their masters' residences for summer occupation, hoping to receive their patronage during the season. This influx of summer visitors nearly doubled the population of the town, and enabled the High Street to support five butchers, three fishmongers, six grocers, three chemists and numerous drapers as well as various other outlets.

In the first half of the twentieth century, the people of the town generally did their shopping locally on the High Street, happy to patronise their local shops. Here, in North Berwick, it was possible to buy all that was required without going up to Edinburgh. But of course the supermarket had not been invented, at least not yet in North Berwick. Women would 'go down the street' for their 'messages' daily - sometimes more than once! Fresh produce was available every day, with most of the food produce made or grown locally. Those who lived in the country would benefit from the daily visit of delivery vans and need only come into town on a Saturday.

The 'Trading Places' exhibition held at the North Berwick Day Centre in 2006 demonstrated that the subject of local shops and the High Street is still very dear to us even though most of our shopping is probably done in an out-of-town supermarket today. Despite that we are still interested in shops: the proprietor, the staff, the goods, the front window, the smells.....

The aim of this book is to gather, preserve and share some of the stories about North Berwick shops and tradesmen of yesteryear. It is a collection of stories and anecdotes from local sources reminiscing about a fast-disappearing way of life, the memories of which are still very vivid in many of our minds and which are surely worth preserving.

John Fergie, 2009

Quality Street

Quality Street, so called because during the late eighteenth and early nineteenth centuries it was seen as *the* place to live. It runs at right angles to the High Street extending from the Lodge in the south to the junction where Forth Street meets Melbourne Place in the north. The complete length of the street was once lined with sycamore and lime trees, the first of which was planted in the mid eighteenth century and which in summer time, would have given this once fashionable quarter of the town a shady continental ambience.

Artist's impression of Quality Street c1850

Quality Street was where the markets were once held with merchants' stances and stalls lining the street, and it is often referred to in old documents as Market Place, Crossgate or Trongait. It may also explain why the south end of the street was so wide, certainly much wider than the High Street. The market cross and Tron were once located near to the Town House.

The current Town House dates from about 1728 and is of two storeys, with a high attic. On the ground floor was a prison cell entered from the High Street with a small dwelling next door. Above, accessed by a steep outside stair, were the Council Chambers and a debtors' prison cell. A clock by Roger Parkinson was added to the bell tower in 1735.

R P Phillimore's impression of the Town House c1905

At the south end of the street is the Lodge, built in the early eighteenth century with later additions, which was home to the Dalrymple family for about two hundred years until 1939 when the house and grounds were taken over by the Town Council.

4

Jenny Elliot's Chip Shop
20 Quality Street

Jenny McNab came to North Berwick in 1929 to go into service at St Colms, eventually rising to position of cook. Jenny soon met and married William Elliot, a barber in Quality Street, setting up home in Kirk Ports. In 1934 when the Elliots were served notice to vacate the flat Jenny went round to see her friend Mr Menzies, the solicitor who worked at the Beehive. He soon found the Elliots accommodation in Quality Street, at No 20, a tenement owned by Mrs Marr, which comprised the ground floor chip shop with three flats over the three storeys above. The Elliots moved into the first floor flat while the top two flats continued under lease to the McAdam and Paxton families. Jenny immediately saw opportunity in the chip shop and set to work.

Andrew Tomasi's Chip Shop in the 1950s

The chips were originally peeled by hand with the fish gutted and filleted by Jenny herself. Eventually, a hand-cranked peeler was purchased but this still meant that the 'eyes' had to be taken out of the potatoes by hand. The two big fryers were coal fired and it was a constant battle to keep the fat at the right temperature. The tatties came from Newmains in Dirleton and the fish came from Aberdeen on the early train each day; white puddings etc came from Edinburgh. The chips were served in a cone wrapped in newspaper but it was possible to sit in too, when fish and chips were served with tea and bread and butter. Afterwards the dishes were washed by Jenny's daughter, Nancy, who had to stand on a box to reach the sink. To increase business Jenny started selling school dinners - soup and a roll - for a shilling a week. The business was sold just after the war to Andrew Tomasi with Jenny retaining the flats and only leasing the shop to Tomasi.

Jenny Hardie and Nancy Chisholm, April 2008

5

Dalrymple Arms Hotel
Quality Street

In 1879 George Burnet took over the tenancy of the Dalrymple Arms Hotel from Mr Charles Fraser. The licensed premises on Quality Street were owned by the Dalrymple family. Mr Burnet kept the tenancy for four years until he purchased the property from Sir Hew Dalrymple for £1300.

Some time later Mr Burnet left for St Andrews; at the same time letting the hotel to Mr McAinsh. After a disagreement, Mr McAinsh acquired the adjoining property, and in 1893 applied for a licence for his property, which he duly received.

DALRYMPLE ARMS HOTEL,
NORTH BERWICK.

CHARLES FRASER.

Breakfast, Luncheon, Dinners, &c.
ON THE SHORTEST NOTICE.

THE WINES, LIQUORS, AND EVERYTHING IN THIS ESTABLISHMENT ARE OF THE BEST QUALITY.

Arrangements have now been made for additional Bed-room Accommodation.

Advert from 1874

McAinsh's Dalrymple Hotel c1890

Imperial Hotel
5/7 Quality Street

However, Mr Burnet's similar application, for his property, was rejected on the grounds that the old hotel was not suitable for the requirements of North Berwick. Mr Burnet speedily had plans drawn up for a new hotel on the same site. In August of 1893 the plans were presented to the inaugural sitting of the Dean of Council Court, which held its first meeting in the Council Chambers with Provost Baillie presiding. The plans were passed, and having taken down his old house, Burnet erected a fine new building at a cost of over £3000. The Imperial Hotel, as it was to be called, consisted of hotel, offices and stables at 5/7 Quality Street and was open for business by 1895. Burnet employed Henry Imrie as his first hotel keeper.

Imperial Hotel   FAMILY AND COMMERCIAL

QUALITY STREET, NORTH BERWICK.
(Situated between East and West Links).

Terms Moderate.   **JOHN BURKE**, Proprietor.

Advert from 1910

Later, in 1903 after a two-year ownership by Donald McPhail, the Imperial Hotel was taken over by James Maguire. When Maguire returned to Edinburgh in 1907 to trade as a spirit dealer in Rose Street, he employed John Burke as his hotel-keeper, letting the stables to William Lockhart, a contractor in the town.

Burke and his wife Annie lived at 9 Balfour Street with their two children, Peggy and Michael. Annie was born at the Heugh Farm and on leaving school trained as a seamstress with William Inglis, the clothier.

Michael left school at 14 and started a club-maker apprenticeship with Ben Sayers on the 18 October 1919 earning 10/- (50p) per week working in the factory at the West Links. At the end of his apprenticeship on the 14 March 1924, Michael left Ben Sayers to go in search of work, firstly to Chingford and then France working in both Aix les Bains and Monte Carlo. In the late 1920s he got a job working as a professional for the Aga Khan who was building a new golf course at Ile Rouse, Corsica. He died in Corsica of enteric fever in 1932 aged 27. He left a pregnant widow whose baby was sadly lost in childbirth.

John Burke worked at the Imperial until early 1911. He died soon after.

Contribution by Mary MacLaren
March 2008

James T. A. Lumsden, Painter
44 Quality Street

James Thomas Aitken Lumsden was born at 18 Shore Street (now Victoria Road) in 1876, one of thirteen children. His father was a slater and plaster. James did a painter's apprenticeship with Willie Laing then in 1922 he started on his own account renting a shop located at 44 Quality Street from Jessie Lockhart. The shop consisted of a front, middle and back shop. The front shop was where James kept cigarettes, pipes, tobacco, post cards and confectionery,

Advert from 1930

which were mainly sold to visitors. The middle shop was where the wall paper was displayed on walls covered in shelves. As well as in the back shop, James stored paint along at his yard on Forth Street, which is now the back of Boots. Customers would come in with a 2lb jam jar and have it filled with paint for one shilling. James was a superb copper-plate sign writer and regularly painted the names of the deceased on coffins, sometimes in gold leaf. His daughters helped run the shop - first Frances and then, when she married, Marie. He also had a number of painters working for him, normally four – six, but sometimes as many as a dozen in the springtime, preparing the large west end villas prior to the start of the season. In those weeks before the season started, Lumsden's painters could earn a small fortune working all the hours God sent, starting as early as 4.00am and working till 8.00pm. The money, of course, was always welcome.

However, disaster overtook them one Wednesday morning in 1933. A fire started about 1.30 am and was soon

Lawrie Lumsden outside his father's shop in 1930s

8

raging throughout the premises. Mr John Gilston, a tenant in one of the top flats above the shop, detected the smell of burning, and on looking out of his window, discovered smoke issuing from Mr Lumsden's shop. He raised the alarm and, obtaining a hose from the nearby garage, applied water to the flames until the arrival of the Fire Brigade. The contents of the shop were of such an inflammable nature, and the fire had taken so firm a hold, that the premises were completely gutted, but thankfully the adjoining property did not suffer. The tenants resident in the houses above were forced to seek shelter with friends until the danger was over. The Fire Brigade left the scene of the outbreak at about 4.30am after rendering good service in preventing the fire from spreading.

Doris, the daughter of Mary Combe, a first floor tenant at No. 42, who had six of her children staying with her that night, recalls being carried down the stairs by Policeman Donald (PC Donald McDonald) and taken by him to Mrs Wallace's for safety. Mary, however, did not know the whereabouts of her 10 year old daughter, and was 'up to ninety', fearing the worst, until they were reunited after the fire was extinguished. Fortu-

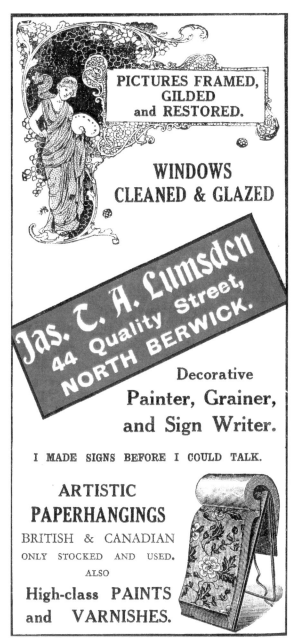

PICTURES FRAMED, GILDED and RESTORED.

WINDOWS CLEANED & GLAZED

Jas. C. A. Lumsden
44 Quality Street, NORTH BERWICK.

Decorative Painter, Grainer, and Sign Writer.

I MADE SIGNS BEFORE I COULD TALK.

ARTISTIC PAPERHANGINGS

BRITISH & CANADIAN ONLY STOCKED AND USED.

ALSO

High-class PAINTS and VARNISHES.

Advert from 1923

nately no one suffered any serious injury. The shop was soon repaired and made good and James continued trading from the premises until 1943.

Contributions by Lawrie Lumsden, April 2008 & Doris McAllister née Combe, October 2008

Lockhart's Dining Tea Rooms
48 Quality Street

Jessie Alan Lockhart's tea rooms were very popular with visitors to the swimming pond wishing a warm drink - particularly those chilled by the icy waters. Unfortunately Jessie's establishment did not have its own private convenience. However patrons of the establishment only need cross the road to the corner of Melbourne Place, to use the Burgh's public convenience under the stewardship of Joanne Soutar. There, one would find immaculate facilities of the highest standards of cleanliness, from the polished terrazzo floor to the burnished copper pipes.

Daisy Young standing at the door of Lockhart's Dining and Tea Rooms at 48 Quality Street in about 1920.

Lockie's Dairy
Quality Street

Lockie's Dairy operated from premises currently occupied by North Berwick Fry. In December 1887 the shop and three bedroomed dwelling above were put up for sale by Public Roup. They sold for the upset price of £450.

Haddingtonshire
North Berwick
TO BE SOLD by Public Roup, within DOWELL'S ROOMS, 18 George Street, Edinburgh, on WEDNESDAY, 21st DECEMBER 1887, at Two o'clock,
(1)   THE SHOP in QUALITY STREET, NORTH BERWICK, presently occupied by Lockie & Coy., Dairy Keepers.
(2)   The DWELLING-HOUSE adjoining, consisting of Sitting-Room, 3 Bedrooms, and Kitchen, and other convenience.
Burgage Holding. Upset Price, £450.
Apply to R. Maxwell Main, Solicitor, Haddington; or Lyle & Wallace, Solicitors, 13 St Andrew Street, Edinburgh, and North Berwick, in whose hands are the Titles and Articles of Roup.

Advert from Courier 16 December 1887

Maggie Gullane's
24 Forth Street

Mrs Gullane had a sweetie shop on Forth Street, where at night, she also sold fish and chips. In the back of the shop was her kitchen with a sink at the window, a cooker and a long scrubbed table on which the chips were made and in the corner a large pan of fat bubbling away on the stove. Strangely, just inside the shop on the left of the counter was a coal-bunker! She had the reputation for making the best chips in the town. Catherine Watt recalls going in after Guides and buying chips with sliced beetroot.

Maggie Gullane outside her shop on Forth Street.

As a girl in the 1920s, Jean Crawford recalls going into the shop on Saturdays, having joined Maggie's Christmas club, with a penny to put towards a selection box. In those days a large selection box could be bought for 2/6d. The shop stocked Dickman's sweets for 4d per quarter pound which Maggie kept in large jars in the shop window. W.M. Duncan's hazelnut chocolate and chocolate drops were other favourites that were kept in the shop. Maggie also sold fruit and vegetables and in the summer would have strawberries and fresh vegetables from the Dales at Seacliff.

Maggie's two daughters, Jessie-Jane and Maggie, ran the shop after their mother's death. It was a great place to hear the news of the day.

Contributions by Jean Crawford & Catherine Watt,
March 2008

Forth Street
4,6 and 20

Eastwards from Maggie Gullane's were two licensed grocers: Dryburgh's at 20 Forth Street on the corner of Viewforth, now a hairdressers, and Dickson's at 4 & 6 Forth Street on the corner of Lorne Square and Forth Street.

Dickson's was run by brother and sister, Jenny and Tom Dickson. It was a low ceiling shop built on land which their father had purchased in 1896. They had a reputation for selling very nice ham. In the 1930s Jenny Dickson moved her business up to the High Street, to the East of the Police Station. Dickson's shop, on Forth Street has now been converted into a house.

In the late 1920s Dryburgh took over the grocery business of David Chalmers who had acquired the business when he married the daughter of the previous proprietor, Mr Stewart. Stewart owned most of the nearby properties including the houses down Viewforth and the property westwards along Forth Street up to and including Maggie Gullane's. The properties then passed to Chalmers and his new wife. Until the late twenties and early thirties the shops on Forth Street thrived, receiving trade from the houses and dwellings nearby such as Russell Square, Melbourne Place, Harbour Terrace and the Gunboat. In those days it was not unusual to have households of ten or more and it was easy for them to access the grocers on Forth Street.

JAMES DICKSON

LICENSED GROCER and
PROVISION MERCHANT

AGENT FOR W. & A. GILBEY'S WINES AND SPIRITS

4 & 6 Forth Street - North Berwick

Established 1874   Telephone No. 48

SALE OF GROUND – On Friday, within the Dalrymple Arms Hotel, the unbuilt-on ground, the property of Mr Adam Young, at the corner of Lorne Lane and Forth Street, having a frontage of about 31 feet to Forth Street and about 33 Feet to the beach, was exposed for sale by public roup at the upset price of £400. The amount rose by bids of £5 to £415, at which sum it was knocked down to Mr James Dickson, grocer. Mr J.W. Hardie was auctioneer.

Top : Advert from c1907
Above : Extract from Haddington
Courier 1 October 1896
Below : Advert from 1922

G. Dryburgh   GROCER AND . .
WINE MERCHANT

20 Forth Street (TELEPHONE No. 113) North Berwick

Every assistance given to Visitors seeking Summer Quarters

Life at the Gunboat on Forth Street in the early 1900s

Viewforth became known locally as Chalmers Wynd because of the number of people from Harbour Terrace who would take the short-cut over the beach to go the Chalmers' shop.

Next door to the Gun Boat was the 'Auld Hoose' which was run by William Liston Blyth. He had taken over the pub in 1897, after the death of Thomas Clark. Clark had overseen the change in properties to the building we know today.

Contribution by Jean Crawford
March 2008

Middle : Original 'Auld Hoose' public house.
Bottom : Later building from mid 1890s

The "Auld Hoose"

FORTH STREET, NORTH BERWICK

WINES AND SPIRITS :: TWO BILLIARD TABLES

ACCOMMODATION FOR CYCLISTS

Proprietor—W. LISTON BLYTH

13

High Street / Westgate

The High Street, until the late nineteenth century, only extended from Quality Street in the east to Kay's Wynd (now Law Road) in the west, and until the early 1930s was of uniform width. The gardens of those properties on the south side once extended all the way back to the churchyard, while, up until the eighteenth century, many properties on the north side had gardens that extended to the beach. Until the Victorian era the properties were irregular in appearance, almost ramshackle, with access to the upper floors on rickety outside stairs. Heating was by means of open fires flued by large 'lums' built out from the buildings.

As properties were extended and redeveloped pends and closes were formed and developed to allow access from the street frontage. The resulting courts and squares, comprising numerous dwellings, housed the growing Victorian population.

In 1893 the High Street was extended westwards with Struth's butcher's shop at 1 Westgate readdressed as 55 High Street. The redevelopment of No.113 by David Horsburgh in 1902, building a tenement comprising of two flats over two shops numbered 113, 115 and 117, marks the extent of the High Street as we know it today. Various redevelopments, particularly in the 1930s, resulted in the renumbering of the street on more than one occasion. Horsburgh's property at 117 is now numbered 133 and occupied by Lockett Bros, wine merchants.

Top Right : High Street looking east decorated to celebrate Queen Victoria's diamond jubilee in 1897.

Bottom Right : Behind the High Street - what the ramshackle development looked like c1880.

James Drummond, Bookseller and Stationer
1 High Street

From about 1870 through to the 1880s, James Drummond rented the shop at 1 High Street and the loft above 1 and 3 High Street from the Burgh Council. As well as the shop in North Berwick he also occupied a shop on Haddington's High Street. Principally a stationer and bookseller, he claimed to have a large stock of toys and fancy goods, 'always in stock and all at Edinburgh prices'. Among the varied goods he sold were the 'Solan' and 'Bass Rock' pens. The former resembled the 'J' pen while the latter was particularly recommended for light writers. Both were available at 6d per box, 7d by post.

Rug and Travelling Straps, Leather Belts, &c.

Fish and Bathing Gown Bags, Vulcanite Bathing Shoes.

J. DRUMMOND,

"CORNER SHOP," NORTH BERWICK.

PENS! PENS! PENS! PENS!

THE "SOLAN" PEN resembles the "J" Pen, but possesses more the nature of a Quill. Boxes, 6d.; by Post 7d.

The "BASS ROCK" PEN is particularly recommended for light writers, as it writes clear and sharp. Boxes, 6d.; by Post 7d.

J. DRUMMOND,
Printer and Manufacturing Stationer,
NORTH BERWICK.

Adverts from 1878

JAS. DRUMMOND,
BOOKSELLER AND STATIONER,
High Street, North Berwick,
(AND HIGH STREET, HADDINGTON.)

Scotsman, Courant, Review, and Daily Mail,
On Sale and punctually delivered.
Books not in Stock, procured on a day's notice.
The Magazines lent out to read.

A LARGE STOCK OF
TOYS AND FANCY GOODS
ALWAYS IN STOCK, ALL AT EDINBURGH PRICES.

Photograph taken in 1884 at the opening of the new water supply. Standing in the doorways of their shops, on the right, are John Walker and James Drummond. Amongst the crowd celebrating are the Rev Mr Anderson, Mr A J Balfour MP, John Whitecross and Provost Peter Brodie. In the centre can be seen a fountain constructed by Baillie Kendall.

John R Whitecross, Grocer and Wine Merchant, 2 High Street

John Runciman Whitecross was a grocer and wine merchant in North Berwick for almost fifty years, establishing his business in the first half of the nineteenth century. He held a seat on the Town Council for nearly forty years and also served a term as Provost. In 1871 Whitecross opened a branch of his shop in the West End. This property was described in the *Haddingtonshire Courier* of 4th August 1871, as being 'very elegant and quite in keeping with', what was then, 'the fashionable part of the burgh. While ornamental in its extreme aspect, its interior is thought to be of great advantage to the residents in the west end quarter, for whose accommodation the premises have been principally erected.'

John R Whitecross has been identified, more than anyone else, with the development of golf in the town. As well as being a consummate player, the winner of many trophies and competitions including the Tantallon Club's Scratch Medal 13 times between 1858 and 1880, he virtually kept up the 'green' at his own expense during this period.

He was a man of vision, and in 1894 installed a telephone connection between his two shops — the first telephone for business purposes in the town — something, which at the time, was expected to set a trend.

JOHN R. WHITECROSS,
FAMILY GROCER & WINE MERCHANT,
NORTH BERWICK,

Begs to intimate that he has opened a BRANCH ESTABLISHMENT at the WEST END of the BURGH. The Premises are large and commodious, and will be found to contain a Select and Varied STOCK of GOODS, suitable for a first-class Family Trade.

Families visiting North Berwick will find his Stock equal in Quality and Variety to the best establishments in the city.

Above : Advert from the Courier 4 August 1871
Below : Whitecross' shop c1885

16

Miller's Sweetie Shop
3 High Street

Robina (Beanie) Miller and her sister moved to North Berwick just before the First World War. Both had been widowed and were keen to be close to their brother William Liston Blyth who was landlord of the Auld Hoose at the time. Beanie and her identical twin daughters, Jessie and May who were born in the Ferry Inn in Alloa in 1896, moved into Seabeach Cottage in Viewforth.

Around about the end of the First World War Beanie and her sister set up a small confectionery business at 3 High Street, probably with some financial help from their brother, selling home-made toffee and tablet. Catherine Watt remembers how they sold 'high class sweets' in white paper bags, far too expensive for her pocket money to stretch to, so she went to Mrs Marr's on Quality Street for liquorice straps and sherbet dabs. The sisters worked very hard to support their respective families and were open six days a week with a half-day on a Thursday – so they could be 'with family'. Locally they were known as the 'Heavenly Twins' and ran the sweetie shop until the thirties. Meanwhile Jessie and May had secured employment in the prestigious Jenners on Princes Street.

Muriel Shiel, May 2008
Catherine Watt, March 2008

East End of High Street, decorated for Coronation of George VI on 12th May 1937, with Jack Shiel's tobacconist shop on the left and Eeles the butchers on the right.

17

Jack Shiel, Tobacconist
6 High Street

Jack Shiel was born in the 1890s and on leaving school gained an apprenticeship with Auld the Joiners. Unfortunately before completing his training he was called up to serve his country in the Great War. After the war his restlessness took him over the Atlantic, working his passage and bunking down in steerage. He landed at Ellis Island and found temporary work as a joiner and farm labourer. Within a year he returned to North Berwick to ask Jessie Miller, the girl he loved, for her hand. Unfortunately she turned him down. He returned to North America travelling in both the United States and Canada ending up in Alaska where he worked as a joiner on the construction of a salmon-canning factory. He suffered the hazards of working in sub-zero temperatures; having to take care with nails which would stick to fingers or other exposed skin in the Artic cold. Again he returned to North Berwick after about a year and again he asked for Jessie's hand. This time she accepted.

SEE THE DISTRICT IN COMFORT
in this most Luxurious 14 Seater CHARA

Pneumatic Tyres on all Wheels, which ensures as Comfortable a Drive as in your own Private Car.

DAILY TOURS.

Private Parties Specially Catered for.

Private Cars for Hire.

Lockups to let.

All Motor Accessories Stocked.

For full particulars and Bookings apply -
Mrs. MILLER,
Confectioner,
High Street,
or
BEVERIDGE & SHIEL
Beach Road Garage,
North Berwick.

Phone 143.

Flyer issued by Shiel's Char-a-banc business c1921

On Jack's return, it was not easy to obtain work, as he had not completed his joiner's training, but he soon set up in business in the early 1920s with his cousin, Lex Beveridge, buying the char-a-banc and car hire business at 3 Beach Road, from Thomas Hunter. The business unfortunately was not a success with the final nail in the coffin coming while Jack and Jessie were on honeymoon. While on a tour to the Lammermuir Hills the driver of the char-a-banc lost control of the vehicle when the brakes failed on the hill down into Garvald. The vehicle was only covered by third party insurance and the loss was too much for the business to sustain.

Once again Lex Beveridge backed Jack when he took over J Renwick's tobacconist business at 6 High Street. Initially Jack and Jessie lived in the back shop, a small room with a double bed, two small armchairs, a fireplace, cooker and sink. Later, probably after a year or so Granny Shiel helped them to buy the flat above the shop. Business was very good before the war as everyone seemed to smoke and getting a

 TOBACCONIST.

Choice Selection of Smokers' Requisites.
PIPES.—B.B.B.—Briars, Loewe's, &c.. Tobacco Pouches, Cigar and Cigarette Cases and Walking Sticks (silver-mounted and plain). Cigarettes, Cigars and Tobaccos, including John Cotton's and other well-known high-class brands. **Good Selection of Local Pictorial Post Cards—R. P. Phillimore's and other leading series.**

J. RENWICK, 6 HIGH STREET (Opposite Town Clock), NORTH BERWICK.

J Renwick's advert from 1913

lighter for one's seventeenth birthday was not unusual. Cigarette packets did not have cellophane wrappers in those days and Jack's eldest son Brian would go through the packets looking for the cigarette cards he required to make up a complete set – always replacing any taken with one of his duplicates. Jack had a number of farmers and west end customers who bought their cigarettes in their own monogrammed packet. As the business prospered Jack was able to move his family to Blythwood on St Andrew Street and run a car - a rarity in those pre-war days. The car, a Morris bought from Gilbert's, was not very powerful and everyone but the driver had to get out to push when it came to a hill. During the summer, from the beginning of May until the end of September, the family would move back into the flat above the shop and let Blythwood out to summer visitors. In the winter they moved back into the family home and Jack let out the flat. The rent money helped pay the rates on the three properties.

During the war Jack was well supplied with rabbits, eggs and vegetables from his farmer customers who were grateful to receive extra cigarettes in those rationed times. Jack served in the Royal Observer Corp and was stationed on top of Castle Hill with William Lamb, the jeweller from Market Place. This meant long nights watching for enemy ship and aircraft movement, which Jack found difficult after standing for eleven hours in his tobacco shop. He left and joined the Auxiliary Fire Brigade.

Jack's youngest son, Michael, took over the business in the late fifties and ran it for a year or so before selling it to John and Thelma Catleugh in 1960.

Muriel Shiel
May 2008

Eeles the Butcher
5 High Street

In 1932, aged 14, Bob Miller applied for a job with George Eeles, the butcher at 5 High Street. Bob's father had recently died and he saw it as his duty to help support the family household. Bob was taken on as message boy and apprentice butcher working beside Bob Bell from Dirleton. Eeles was owned and run by the then Provost George Eeles, who in Bob's opinion, was the only man who could really count. He could run his eye up a column of figures - pounds, shillings and pence - and write down the total, without checking, knowing that it was correct.

One of Bob's duties was to go around the regular customers at the east of the town and collect their orders. Meanwhile Sandy Greig, Eeles' nephew, would go around collecting orders from the west end. One of the cooks up the avenue who worked in the Nether Abbey Hotel would, as well as buying meat from Eeles, sell back the dripping after cooking.

Sandy also slaughtered the animals up at the abattoir. At that time, Bob Hannan was caretaker at the slaughterhouse and Bill Paxton his assistant. Bert Young a local general contractor transported the carcases down to the shop in his lorry. Like all the butchers in the town, Eeles leased land for his own beasts, sometimes the Glebe or possibly up at Abbotscroft.

Turkeys came from Fenton Barns, chickens came from the Heugh Farm and rabbits from a game dealer. The chickens were plucked and the rabbits skinned in the back shop. It was not unusual for customers to come in to have their game skinned or feathered although Eeles did not sell game, as it had no licence.

When he first started, Bob, had to go next door to Brodie's the bakers if hot water was required as there was none in Eeles. Eeles used to sell meat to Brodies for their pies and customers would bring in an enamel dish which Eeles would fill with meat and take it next door to Brodie's who would put on the pastry and cook it.

Bob Miller April 2008

View of High Street looking west c1950

Brodies the Bakers
9 -13 High Street

Gladys Porteous started working in Brodies in 1945 after leaving school at 15. Her family were living at the Rhodes Cottages, her father being a horseman, and she would cycle to and from work also going home for dinner. Later when the Logans came to stay at the Rhodes she and Peggy would chum each other as she was working at Alexander James. At that time Brodie's was owned by the Gordon brothers, Ralph and Eddie. Gladys' pay on the first week was 10/- and thereafter she got 15/- and worked six days with a half-day on a Thursday. She also remembers getting a half-day on VE day too. Her duties included serving, tidying up and making up orders for the van. In those days a half loaf cost 4½d.

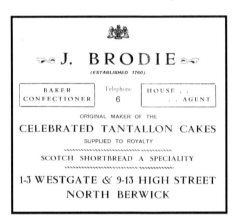

Advert from 1920

The van was driven by Dod Oliver and Katie Anderson would go out with him and help. Most of the big houses got daily deliveries when they were occupied during the season. The rest of the time the van was out on its regular runs either in North Berwick or out in the country. Some of the owners of the big houses were very kind to the staff: Miss Grieve of 'The Latch' would send her chauffeur round at Christmas with presents, sometimes toiletries, to be shared amongst the girls.

Before the shop opened at eight o'clock those 'in the know' would go up the vennel to the yard at the back of the shop where one of the bakers, possibly Harry Richardson, who lived in Victoria Road, would sell fresh rolls straight out the oven. The smell of fresh bread was wonderful. Eddie Gordon and Willie Hutchison were the other bakers who worked at Brodie's during the time Gladys worked there. Willie had worked for Haig's in Dirleton, where he lived, and once they had been taken over by the Co-op he started at Brodie's cycling in every day on his drop-handle bike. The ovens in those days were heated with coke. As well as rolls the bakers made crusties - a small well fired loaf; a high loaf which when sliced looked like a lop-sided 'm'; and ring loaves - cylindrical loaves with ridges showing where to slice.

The upper bakehouse, accessible by an outside staircase in the back yard, was where the cakes and other confectionery were made. Ralph Gordon worked up there with Jock Tait and Bob Lawrence. Bob who stayed in Market Place did all the fancy decoration. Doughnuts, cream cookies, scones, and meringues were amongst the produce made as well as wedding cakes, but the speciality was Tantallon Teacakes. They were famous the world over and even members of the Royal family were partial to them. They were made with a shortbread recipe, shaped in a circle with a scalloped edge and had a dusting of castor sugar on top. At Christmas they made another favourite: shortbread with an iced picture of the Bass and a small boat. This was an ideal present to be sent to friends and relatives all over the world.

Also upstairs was a tearoom that the public could access by stairs from the High Street. Here, customers could indulge in afternoon and high teas. Most of the food was cooked by Ralph in the kitchen beside the upper bakehouse.

Gladys Miller née Porteous
April 2008

Commercial Hotel
15/17 High Street

In March 1890 Francis Edington, well known proprietor of the Commercial Hotel (currently called the County Hotel) disposed of the business and property to Henry White, and his wife, who, according to the *Courier* of 14 March 1890, came to the town excellently well recommended. Mr White had for many years been butler to Sir George Warrender Bt of Lochend. The property comprised the coach house and stables on Kirk Ports as well as the building on the High Street.

In 1893, the Courier reported how William Conway, Balgone Barns, was charged with having falsely represented himself as a *bona fide* traveller in the Commercial Hotel. The accused pled guilty having apparently stated to the hotelier that he had come from Brownrigg. He was fined 5 shillings with the option to serve 5 days imprisonment.

In 1907 the Commercial Hotel was taken over by John Wilson, who had until then been proprietor of the Temperance Hotel in Dunbar, trading under the name of Wilson's Hotel. It was reported at the time that John Wilson was well fitted for his new undertaking having extensive experience in management of hotels over a long number of years.

The stables in Kirk Ports were let to David Runciman who ran a successful riding school there. He continued in business until 1929 when his riding school was taken over by Thomas Moncur of the Belford Riding Academy.

John Wilson sold the hotel in 1933 to Hugh Harper, who kept it for a couple of years before selling on to John Campbell Cameron.

Advert from 1920

Day's, Photographer
19/21 High Street

George Day established his photography business in Dunbar in 1918. Then in partnership with Miss Beatrice Govan he established a studio in North Berwick at 5 Market Place in the late 1920s before later moving, on his own account, to 19 High Street in 1946. His son George, who was born just after the Great War and educated in Dunbar, started work in his father's photography business as soon as he left school. George did mostly freelance press photography for the likes of the 'Bulletin' and 'People's Journal' with all the processing and developing done in-house. George and his son would cover anything that was topical at that time, for instance when the whales were washed up at Thorntonloch, Dunbar. Commission work was carried out for postcard printers like Valentine's of Dundee. When Valentine's wanted pictures of sea birds, Freddie Marr took young George out to the Bass Rock to take the photographs. When the presswork dried up the Days started doing weddings, christenings and other local events.

Contribution by George Day, April 2008

Top : Day's photograph studio at 19/21 High Street
*   c1950*
Middle Right : Day and Govan's postcard of Joe
*   Anderson's Entertainers in 1927.*
Bottom Right : George Day's photograph of the
*   stranded whales at Thorntonloch*

John Wightman, Furnishing Ironmonger
23/25 High Street

On the 28 May 1704, the land and property, on which 23/25 High Street stand today, were acquired by William Grahame and his wife Elizabeth Reid from Sir Hew Dalrymple. The property, including the yards at the back, extended from the King's High Street in the north to the Kirk yard in the south, and bounded by the tenements of John Heburn, Captain of the Bass, on its east and west boundaries. The cost of the property was £150 and 14 shillings, *english,* about £1800 *scots.*

In 1719, the property was conveyed by William and Elizabeth to their son, George, also a slater, subject to an annuity payment of £136, *scots,* to his sisters, Ann and Marion. By 1745, the property had been conveyed to George's daughter Elizabeth, who subsequently married David Dall, Schoolmaster at Inchtower and afterwards Yester.

In 1808, Elizabeth, by then a widow, conveyed the property to her son James, her youngest son who was merchant in the town, reserving for herself an annuity of £200 from the estate. Two of Elizabeth's other sons found their fortune in Edinburgh. Thomas established a firm of chartered accountants, Dall & Miller, in Hill Street and William traded in glass and chinaware from shop premises at 4 Hanover Street. The present shop at 23/25 High Street, North Berwick with houses above, was built by James in 1815. During the building of an extension to the property in the early 1900s, bottles and newsprint from 1815 were found in the old masonry.

Advert from Haddingtonshire Courier June 1868

James was one of the partners in the firm of Croall, Dall, Brodie & Co., which established the 'Original North Berwick Coach' in 1830. The coach would leave North Berwick for the capital at 7.00am returning from Edinburgh at 4.00pm. The fare - three shillings inside and two shillings outside - for a journey performed in good time, with racing strictly prohibited. By the mid 1800s James had also formed a partnership with his son, James, trading as James Dall & Son. This business encompassed the merchants and newly established house agency businesses and in 1857 the agency for the British Linen Bank. James Snr lived in the house above the shop until his death in 1866. Unfortunately his son, James, survived him by less than two years.

The property then effectively passed to Janet, James Jnr's daughter, who was granted a life rent to the house with the shop and other property retained under the control of the late James Dall's trustees, Dall & Miller. From 1869 the property was let to John Grieve & Son, merchant and house agent in the town. In July 1878, Grieve, a member of the Police Commission, complained to the Police Commission who occupied the adjoining offices, that something must be done about the Council's proposal to renumber his shop, since he had just issued hundreds of circulars previous to this being done. The Commission instructed the Clerk of the Town Council to write to Grieve, regretting that he had any cause for complaint, explaining that no change would now be made to the numbering. Other members of the Police Commission at the time included Francis Edington, hotelier; James Herriot, cabinet-maker; James Lumsden, slater; John Bell, coach proprietor; John R. Whitecross, merchant; and Alex Sandilands, butcher. The running of the business was eventually taken over by Jessie Grieve, a spinster and sole partner. Then in 1898, John Wightman, who previously trained as an ironmonger in Spittal, took over the business interests of Grieve.

In 1902 the property at 23/25 and the adjacent property at 27, on its westmost boundary, were put up for sale by Public Roup. Both properties were purchased by John Wightman for £2000. John retained 23/25 and the cobbled floored stable on the Kirk Ports boundary and sold off the balance of the property to John Walker, bootmaker, for £500. Walker immediately employed Richard Whitecross, joiner and contractor, to build a new property on the site, demolishing the old eighteenth century building.

Top : Advert from 1922

Above : Advert from Haddingtonshire Courier 1902

John Wightman and his two sons David and Robert standing at the entrance to No.23 c1910

Advert from c1930

John Wightman sold a wide variety of garden tools and implements including Coldwell's Gem hand mower (seen above on the left of the doorway) manufactured in Newburgh, New York by the Coldwell Lawn Mower Company. Household and agricultural goods as well as sporting requisites for the shooter and fisher, were his three other main areas of business. Fencing wire and coir yarn, both kept in the wooden hut in the back yard, were big sellers to his farming customers as were his shotgun cartridges, which he made himself on the premises. Household goods included kitchen utensils, mats, brushes and paint. John Wightman was also able to hire goods to his customers, as can be seen from the painted sign by his shop entrance. It was not unknown for visitors while staying in their summer residence to be caught short of a hipbath, a double bed or even a canteen of cutlery for the unexpected overnight guests. He also acted as house agent for a modest number of clients.

Staff during the period before the Second War, included Bobby Neil, Bertie Birnie from Dirleton and John Grieve, a bachelor from Hawick, who was no relation to his previous namesake. When John Wightman died in 1938 the business was taken over by his wife Jane, who continued to run the business until her death in 1946. In 1947, the business and shop were bought by John Grieve.

Contribution by John Wightman
February 2009

David Wood, Draper
27 High Street

Next door to Wightman's, at number 27, was David Wood's draper shop which he opened in 1907, initially renting the shop from John Walker. The previous tenant was Robert Colledge who ran a grocery business from the shop since its establishment in 1902. David Wood traded there for many years with the help of his assistant, Miss Rubina Flora Dempster.

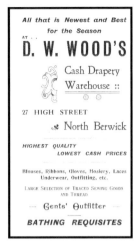

All that is Newest and Best for the Season

AT . . .

D. W. WOOD'S

Cash Drapery
Warehouse ::

27 HIGH STREET

& North Berwick

HIGHEST QUALITY
LOWEST CASH PRICES

Blouses, Ribbons, Gloves, Hosiery, Laces
Underwear, Outfitting, etc.

LARGE SELECTION OF TRACED SEWING GOODS
AND THREAD

— Gents' Outfitter —

BATHING REQUISITES

Advert from c1930

In the days between the wars the shop was kept busy with the demands of growing families. It was piled high with goods for sale and there was a long pulley which hung above Miss Dempster's head, at the point where she was serving, which was draped with undergarments, corsets and that sort of thing. Other goods for sale, all wrapped up with paper and string were kept high up on shelves, which she accessed by climbing up a ladder. She would slowly untie the string, unwrap the paper then reveal the box's contents which usually matched the customer's enquiry. Then having secured a sale, but before receiving payment, she would re-wrap the box, tie it up with string and slowly replace it on its shelf. The ritual was always the same even when the sale was only for a 1d packet of pins. A customer had to be prepared to wait an eternity to conclude a purchase.

When Mr Wood died in 1942 he left Miss Dempster the business and property, which he had purchased some years earlier, in his will.

Always a trifle eccentric, she became ever more so as the years wore on: she would not open the shop until the afternoon; she would not change the front window display which included knitting patterns with curled corners and yellowed with age. She would stay open quite late at night, sitting in her thread-bare gabardine coat. On winter evenings she would sit in the dark, since her only means of light was from a bicycle lamp, which she would only use when a customer came in. The shop did have a gaslight but she did not believe in extravagance.

Jean Fraser remembers Miss Dempster telling her that she was born in Newtongrange and that on the day of her birth, her mother had three coffins in the parlour of the house. Evidently there had been a mining accident and her father, brother aged 14, and an uncle had all been killed. Perhaps this was an explanation for her strange and eccentric ways.

Contributions by Jean Crawford March 2008 and
Alistair and Irene Stewart June 2009

Footnote from the Scottish Mining Website: 'The Mauricewood Pit fire broke out at noon on the 5 September 1889. The fire resulted in the loss of 63 lives. Most of the bodies, including William Dempster aged 31(uncle), Robert Dempster aged 37(father) and Robert jun aged 14(brother) were not recovered until March 1890.' Rubina Flora Dempster was born 5 March 1890.

John Walker, Bootmaker
27 High Street

John Walker, a part time postman, established his boot making business on North Berwick's High Street in 1877. The original shop was at 3 High Street, next door to James Drummond the printer and bookbinder, and below the Subscription Library and Reading Room which was itself established in 1827. At that time the Library was under the stewardship of George MacGregor, the librarian, who lived at Kay's Wynd.

JOHN WALKER,

BOOT AND SHOE MAKER,

HIGH STREET, NORTH BERWICK.

Repairs Neatly and Promptly Executed.

Advert from 1878

The whole building was let by the Magistrates and Council of the Burgh of North Berwick, by one Robert Lyle. The Walker family rented a house and garden in the Westgate, which at that time ran from Law Road westwards. John was married to Jessie Telfer and they had 6 children: 3 boys and 3 girls.

Between the 1870s and the early years on the new century the business and family moved a couple of times: firstly in the 1880s to a house and shop at 41 High Street leased from Andrew Lockhart the carter and then in the early 1890s to 14/16 High Street which was leased from Margaret Henderson the wife of T W Henderson master mariner. In 1902 the property at 27 High Street was purchased from John Wightman for £500. Walker contracted Peter Whitecross to demolish the old property and build a new three storey tenement

John Walker Jnr decorating his shop at 27 High Street for the 1911 Coronation. Upstairs at the window are his sons Clarence or Frank and James and John

28

consisting of a shop with two houses above with a further shop/ workshop. The family used the shop and first floor flat and let out the second floor flat to John Swan, a butcher, and the workshop to R Colledge.

John Walker junior, the middle child of John and Jessie, married Agnes Peden, a descendant of Alexander Peden, a leading Covenanter who was imprisoned on the Bass Rock with John Blackadder. John and Agnes had 7 children - 5 boys and 2 girls. All the boys joined the army and went on to fight for their country in the Great War. Two of the sons were killed in France, Clarence the third oldest was killed on the first day of the Somme and Walter died the following year, 1917. Later that year their father, John died - it was said, of a broken heart having lost 2 of his sons.

On his father's death, Frank, the fourth eldest, was recalled from the front in France, to carry on the family business and support the family - his mother, two sisters and the widow of Clarence who had given birth to a daughter, Clarissa, in 1915.

Soon after Frank's return to North Berwick he met Edith Everitt, a seamstress who worked for the Innes family. The Innes family had a summer residence on West Bay Road and it was during one summer visit that Frank met Edith. It was about this time that Frank decided to sell the family firm to a small multiple, letting the shop to the firm of Cuthbert & Sons. Soon after, Frank married Edith near her hometown in Norfolk and after their honeymoon they set sail for Quebec on the 'Empress of France' where Frank got a job as manager of a farming co-operative. There soon followed the birth of their first son in 1921. However the climate did not suit the young family and they returned to the UK after two or three years. On the family's return, Frank found a job repairing shoes at the Elephant and Castle in London.

Frank also made arrangements to buy back the shoe business in North Berwick which incurred the family considerable debt that took many years to clear. On returning to North Berwick in 1924, Frank and his family took up residence at 4 Quality Street. Other members of the family were still living above the shop at 27 High Street with the top flat occupied by Miss Watt, the district nurse, and her mother. When the Watts moved to St Andrew Street in 1926, Frank and his family moved to the top flat. The flat was lit by means of gas but unusually for the time it had the latest in bathrooms, a novelty in those days when many families bathed in a tin bath in front of the fire, if indeed they bathed at all. There was a garden 40 or 50 yards long with a large wooden gate on to Kirk Ports.

Like a large number of families in North Berwick the Walkers let out the whole or part of the flat during the season. If the whole flat was let a room had to be taken elsewhere or if only part of the flat was let they were confined to one room, cooking on a gas ring. The common greeting on the street in the Spring was 'Are ye let yet?' Clarence Walker recalled spending summers in various flats nearby – at the Siveses in Fenton Cottage, the Murrays in Melbourne Place and the Wilsons across the road at 28 High Street although he often slept on a bed in his father's workshop amid old shoes, leather parings, the smell of gas, stale tobacco smoke and the inevitable dust.

During the war when there was an air-raid, the Walkers would shelter in a cellar-like space between the workshop and the front shop where the leather hides were kept. The makeshift shelter's roof was the underside of the concrete stairway leading to the flats above. There was no ventilation and the smell of leather and candles was not altogether health-enhancing. If there had been a direct hit there would have been no escape. On one occasion there was an almighty bang followed by the sound of falling objects in the front shop. German bombers had been dropping anti-shipping mines in the Firth of Forth and some had been washed on to the beaches, with one exploding on contact with the rocks nearby.

Fenton Cottage, Kirk Ports. Now demolished.

In 1949 Frank and Edith Walker moved along to 41/43 High Street, taking over the house and shop of the Balden sisters. The property at 27 was taken over by the Edinburgh Savings Bank, with the flat above let to the manager, Ian McAlpine.

Contribution by
Clarence Walker

Spring 2000

Above : 47 High Street c1950

Thomas Wilson, Printer and Stationer
The White House, 33 High Street

T. A. WILSON, Printer, Stationer, and Newsagent,

High Class Stationery. Fancy Goods of every description. Large Selection of Local Views. China, Glass & Earthenware (large stock). Crest China (large assort ment. . . ☞ Sole Agent for Goss.

"The White House," No. Berwick.

Stationers . .	
Booksellers . .	Newspapers, Periodicals, etc., delivered to all parts of town
Newsagents . .	

THE WHITE HOUSE
(W. KERR, Proprietor)

NORTH BERWICK
EL. 54

PRINTING

SATISFACTION - SERVICE

~ Satisfaction—We guarantee entire satisfaction in all work entrusted to us.

~ Service—Our staff of skilled crafts-men and modern machines enable us to carry out all our work efficiently and speedily and give the very best service available at most reasonable prices.

White House Printing Office
Commercial and General Printers

THE ONLY PRINTING OFFICE IN NORTH BERWICK

Thomas Wilson started trading in the White House, at 33 High Street, in 1910, taking over the tenancy of the property from George C Murray, the stationer. As well as a stationer, Wilson was a newsagent, printer and publisher. Wilson printed billheads, billposters, whist drive cards and any other printed material local clubs and societies required. He also published a regular list of summer visitors to the town. In addition to his extensive stock of postcards for sale, he also sold fancy goods including 'Goss China'!

Top Left: Advert from 1913
Above : Advert from 1938

Above : c1900 High Street looking east with the White House of Mr Murray on the right. His range of postcards and local views can be seen at the shop doorway. His printing works were at the rear of the shop and could be accessed from Kirk Ports. Two properties along from the White house is a low pantiled property which was demolished by John Walker in 1902.

Wilson,
Clothier and Tailor, Confectioners and Restaurateurs
26/28 High Street

JOHN J. WILSON

Exclusive Gent's Outfitter

28 High Street
NORTH BERWICK

Above and Below : Adverts from 1922
Right : Wilson's shop at 28 High Street c1950

From about 1920, John Wilson owned the property at 26/28 High Street, now the Co-op funeral directors. The shop was divided down the middle by a wooden partition with John, known locally as 'Sweetie Jock' trading as a gentlemen's outfitter from one half of the shop, and his two spinster sisters, Agnes and Margaret, operating out of the other half, as a sweetie shop and tearoom. They stayed in the flats above the shop, which were entered from the Cat's Close.

Previously, the property had been owned by Lena Blair, who let the shop to Mary and Catherine Cruickshanks. The National Telephone Co. Ltd. let the first floor from about 1897, from where they operated North Berwick's first telephone exchange.

Contribution by Sandy Struth, April 2008

A. & M. WILSON

Confectioners and
Restaurateurs . .

28a High St., North Berwick

Parties

Catered

For

John Macintyre, Chemist
34 High Street

John Macintyre, known locally as 'Pa', opened his first shop, in North Berwick, in 1881. He started renting a shop at 9 Quality Street from John Whitecross, trading as a chemist and druggist, but soon moved to more central premises in the High Street around 1890. Originally from Bonar Bridge in Sutherland, he trained as a chemist with Duncan and Flockhart in Edinburgh. To train as a chemist in those days it was necessary to be articled to a dispensing chemist, and prior to the First War, most of those who trained as chemists were male.

'Pa' Macintyre was a strict disciplinarian but an excellent mentor who gave a thorough training. There were no manufactured medicines then. The pills, tonics and ointments were all made by hand. The doctor's prescription would inform the dispenser of the actual quantities of compounds for each medicine, whether pill or liquid. For pills the ingredients were first mixed into a paste and then moulded to shape and then counted into a little cardboard box. The tonics and cough medicines, once mixed, were poured into bottles, wrapped in white paper and sealed with wax. Miss Law, Pa's bookkeeper, was there to ensure that the medicines were wrapped properly, and she taught the apprentices to wrap up the little parcels excellently.

Above: John Macintyre's chemist shop decorated for the Coronation of Edward VII in 1902
Below : Advert from 1922

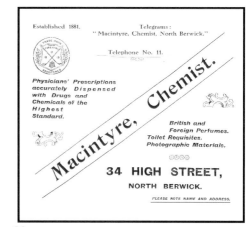

Established 1881.

Telegrams :
" Macintyre, Chemist, North Berwick."

Telephone No. 11.

Physicians' Prescriptions accurately Dispensed with Drugs and Chemicals of the Highest Standard.

Macintyre, Chemist.

British and Foreign Perfumes.
Toilet Requisites.
Photographic Materials.

34 HIGH STREET,
NORTH BERWICK.

PLEASE NOTE NAME AND ADDRESS.

The other string to Macintyre's bow was his lemonade and soft drinks factory situated in Forth Street Lane. It was in this factory, employing up to 20 workers, that his celebrated table waters were produced: lemonade, cola, cream soda and of course his famous ginger beer. Although they were sold mainly in East Lothian it was possible to buy the soft drinks in Glasgow and even over the border.

In the basement of the shop was a photographic department in which Macintyre kept film and developing chemicals. Photography was becoming very popular, particularly from the early 1920s, and the shop would be very busy in the summer with wealthy visitors like Sir John Lavery.

Above : Murray Stewart, Essie Robertson and Rowena Bisset standing outside Macintyre's shop at 34 High Street in c1925
Below : Advert from c1922

In 1915 Rowena Bisset was taken on as a trainee earning £1 a month. She was Macintyre's first female apprentice, and probably one of many girls, across the country, who were taken on to train as chemists, due to the shortage of young men, who were being recruited for the front. Rowena, the daughter of Sergeant Andrew and Barbara Bisset, was born in 1901 - the second of three daughters. Her elder sister Nancy went to work as book keeper for Mr Cowan, at George Shiel, while Sheila, when she was old enough trained to become a teacher.

Unfortunately Rowena was unable to complete her training due to the early death of her father, which placed financial hardship upon her mother. This prevented Rowena taking her professional exams as payment was required. However, Rowena continued to work for 'Pa' until 1929, when she left to get married.

Some of the other locals who trained as chemists with 'Pa' were Geordie Orr, Murray Stewart and Essie Robertson, daughter of the local blacksmith. Essie eventually went on to open her own pharmacy in London.

Macintyre was a member of the Town Council for almost 30 years and was Provost for 20 years between 1899 and 1919, longer than anyone else. During his term in office many local projects came into being including: the swimming pond, the tennis courts and the new gas works.

When Macintyre found out, in the mid 1920s, that Boots intended opening a branch in North Berwick he quickly opened a west end branch at 23 Westgate in 1927 which was sufficient to keep the large multiple out of the town.

John Macintyre died in June 1928 and his chemist shops were taken over by Fletcher McIntosh. The lemonade business was eventually taken over by Globe. In 1934 the chemist business changed hands again when it was taken over by Boots Cash chemists (Northern) Ltd.

Barbara Montgomery, January 2009

Above : Provost John Macintyre
Right : Advert from 1894 (sic)

Henderson's Newsagents
44 High Street

I started work at Henderson's Newsagents and stationers when I left school at 14 in 1939. The business, previously run by Catherine Bertram and Margaret Hill, was owned by Bob and Meg Henderson who lived in the upstairs flat with their son and two daughters. I got the 7.00am bus from Dirleton where I lived with my parents. The bus got in about ten past seven and I started work at quarter past, returning home on the bus at 5.00pm. The return ticket cost about 2d.

First of all I would sweep the shop floor and then Mr Henderson would drive us up to the station in his royal blue and black Lanchester car to collect the papers: 'Scotsman', 'Mail', 'Express', 'Telegraph' etc. When we got back to the shop I helped Mr Henderson make up the rounds for the three paperboys and all the other orders. Then I would accompany Mr Henderson up Dirleton Avenue, York Road and the West

ROBERT H. HENDERSON
Bookseller, Stationer, Printer

LIBRARY CONTAINS THE LATEST NOVELS

Printing & Diestamping at keenest prices

High-class Leather and Fancy Goods.   Fountain Pens and Cigarettes in good variety.

Genuine Clyde-built Yachts.   Agent for Puller's, Perth

SERVANTS' REGISTRY.   SHIPPING AGENT

MORNING AND EVENING PAPERS DELIVERED

44 HIGH STREET, NORTH BERWICK
Telephone 351

Advert from 1930s

End to deliver the papers to the big houses. Once the deliveries had been done, Mrs Henderson gave me my breakfast in the flat upstairs.

Afterwards, my duties were mainly general domestic housework: cleaning the flat hoovering, dusting and cleaning, even washing the attic dormer windows, inside and out. Mrs Henderson would make me crawl along the little parapet to clean the outside of the windows. 'Don't look down, Amy!' Mrs Henderson would shout. I had no intention of doing so, I was petrified! I would be shaking when she handed out to me a ruler and chamois and was told 'Don't miss the corners.' My dad would have been livid if he had known.

If the shop was really busy I was expected to help behind the counter, assisting Miss Birdie Himsworth and Miss Frances Melrose. As well as newspapers, the shop sold diaries, leather goods (wallets), calendars, books, comics, pens and other stationery goods. We also sold model yachts, which were very popular during the summer when competitions were held on the boating pond.

I remember delivering papers on Christmas day 1940. The snow was over the pedals of the delivery bike and falling really heavily. One of the 'toffs' up the Avenue gave me a real swearing because his 'Scotsman' had got wet. It really upset me. A little later, down Strathearn Road, Mr Boyd, who lived in Greenpark, came out and wished me a 'Merry Christmas' and gave me a 10/- note. I was so happy.

Amy Imrie
April 2008

E & H Balden, Drapers and Milliners
41/43 High Street

During the late 1880s and early 1890s, Miss Elizabeth Kerr Balden and Miss Helen Sinton Balden, sisters and spinsters, ran a Milliner and drapery business at 20 High Street. At that time they were also agent for McNab, Dyers, Inglis Green. In 1893 they

moved across the street to what was then 41/43 High Street, renting the house, shop and cellar from the Trustees of Alex Grieve, eventually purchasing the property in about 1910. They were extremely well-to-do and spoke with a 'posh' accent. Catherine Watt can recall her mother buying a hat which was covered in white feathers from one of the Misses Balden – it was often referred to as wearing the 'full hen.' On one occasion, while climbing Waverley Steps, the wind caught Mrs Watt's hat and carried it on to the road in Princes Street, where a large passing Clydesdale horse stood right on top of it, cutting it with its shoe. On returning to North Berwick Mrs Watt engaged the services of Miss Balden who duly repaired the hat with a piece of ribbon.

Lawrie Lumsden can remember his mother being ushered through to the back shop to have her '*wideness*' measured.

Contributions by Catherine Watt & Lawrie Lumsden
March 2008

J P Marshall, Drapers
44 High Street

At Marshall's draper's shop at 44 High Street, customers had to climb down two steps to get into the shop. When Mr Marshall had a sale, people used to joke, 'Marshall's trousers are coming down.' The property was demolished in the 1930s and replaced by the Police Station which was previously located in Victoria Road.

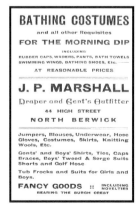

Above : Advert from 1922

Left : High Street looking east with 41/43 first right and 44 first left c1900

Archibald Denholm, Joiner and Undertaker
45/47 & 110 High Street

Archibald Denholm was born in 1851. His father Andrew was a carter in the Cramond area, transporting coal for Bunyan of Haymarket and others. So valued was Andrew to the Bunyan firm, that when they heard of Archibald's desire to train as a joiner, they organised his apprenticeship with an established joiner and cabinet-maker, and purchased a complete set of tools for him.

In the 1880s Archibald Denholm moved down to North Berwick from Edinburgh eventually obtaining work with Peter Whitecross, building contractor, 45 Melbourne Place. In 1906 when Peter Whitecross retired, Archibald and John Murray took over the workshops renting the property from Whitecross. A few years later they also rented Whitecross' office and store at 88 High Street.

By this time Archibald was the father to five sons and five daughters and there was some degree of pressure on the sons to join the family business. Alex had already emigrated to Canada and Robert had started work for Mr Wallace, in the Town Clerk's office. The outbreak of war in 1914 changed everything. The three eldest sons - Jock, Duncan and Alex - who by then had returned from Canada, were all called up. Fearing the worst, being called up to serve in the family firm, Robert escaped at 17 years of age and ran away from home to join the Royal Scots 8th Battalion 1/8. Fortunately all four brothers returned home to North Berwick.

After the war Alex and Duncan emigrated to Australia, taking up positions as golf professionals - a sport at which they and Robert excelled. Robert also longed for a career in golf but his future lay with the family firm beside his brother Jock and his father who had been trading on his own account since 1917.

Above : Advert from c1914
Below : Archibald Denholm 1920s

Jock went about town on his bicycle jobbing and pricing estimates while Robert and George Bee, their brother-in-law, worked mainly at the workshop. When a job was 'urgent' it was not unusual for a client up the 'Avenue' to send a taxi for Jock, thereby ensuring their needs were satisfied forthwith. If a job required more material than could be carried on a bike, Adam Young, a local carter, would be hired to make the necessary delivery.

Jock and Robert took the opportunity to buy the shop, store and workshop at 45/47 High Street in 1936, one year after their father's death. This provided them with a shop frontage and large workshops at the rear, all the way back to Kirk Ports. At one time a hand operated mortice machine was their only piece of technology. By this time they also owned the office at 110 (previously 88) High Street and the two flats above, where the brothers and their families stayed.

Above :49/51 High Street c1950
Below : Workshops at the rear of 49/51 during the coronation celebrations 1937

Robert gradually spent more time developing the antique side of the business, travelling to both Edinburgh and Glasgow with a large brown suitcase to purchase new stock, particularly silverware. He would return home and open the case to show his family the latest pieces he had purchased from the Jewish traders in the city. During the war the shop was frequented by Polish soldiers anxious to buy silver to take home. One day an elegant lady from Edinburgh purchased a piece of silverware. On asking her details in order to complete the invoice, Robert was surprised to learn her name was Miss Bunyan. Further enquires confirmed that she was indeed related to the Coal merchant at Haymarket. Explaining the purpose of his enquiry, Robert immediately discounted the cost of a set of joiner's tools from the account, much to the surprise and delight of the lady.

The office at 110 was manned by Miss Mailer, and later by Rowena Montgomery, who was responsible for the mail, telephone and accounts. Robert's young sons would often come down to use the typewriter, when they needed to type up the school rugby teams. Since the office was also where the coffins were retained, sometimes loaded, the young Denholms would be sitting typing up the teams with one eye on the paper and the other on the coffin lid!

For a funeral, Jock and Robert would dress in their tails and lum hats and take their place in the funeral car, usually supplied by Dod Gilbert. It was important for the town's undertakers to keep their ear to the ground for any clue of an impending death. Each of the town's undertakers, Aulds, Himsworths and Denholms, had an inkling as to what business was likely to come their way. Therefore early knowledge ensured that preparations could be made as soon as possible. On one occasion when returning from a funeral, Jock instructed the hearse driver to take a detour along Glenburn to see if the blinds were drawn at a particular house!

Offices at 110 High Street 1937

Jock and Robert continued to trade until their retirement in the early 1960s.

Contribution by George Denholm
October 2008

Findlay, Bootmaker
51/53 High Street

Mrs Findlay's boot shop was at the corner of Law Road and the High Street. She was a stout elderly lady who wore a black apron and glasses. The door bell would jangle when you went in, then there was a wait while you heard the stairs creak as she descended slowly from above. You felt a bit ashamed when all you wanted was a pair of laces but she would take your money and retreat to her eyrie above.

Jean Crawford
March 2008

A.C. Laing, Tobacconist
49 High Street

William Laing and his brother travelled down from Ellon in Aberdeenshire to Dunbar in about 1880. They found premises in the town and started trading as painters and decorators, a trade they had learned from their father, Alexander, who ran his own painters' business in Ellon. The brothers endured a stormy relationship which ended about 1884, with William and his young family leaving Dunbar, and moving to North Berwick. In North Berwick, William found rented premises, comprising a house and shop in Quality Street, firstly at 9 and then at 44. In 1900 he and his family moved to the Dalrymple Buildings renting a house and shop at 78 High Street. Soon one of his elder daughters, Annie, was running the shop. In fact he had nine children: four sons - Alexander, William, Jock and James and five daughters - Annie, Queenie, Ella, Edith and Daisy. As well as dealing with enquiries and accounts for the painters business, Annie also ran a successful tobacconist business from the shop.

In the early 1930s they moved shop, renting the shop at 49 High Street from Jane Findlay. Annie was having to spend more time with her father who was by that time suffering from poor health. Annie's brother,

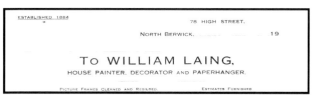

ESTABLISHED 1884   78 HIGH STREET.
                          NORTH BERWICK.   19

To WILLIAM LAING,
HOUSE PAINTER. DECORATOR AND PAPERHANGER.

PICTURE FRAMES CLEANED AND REGILDED.   ESTIMATES FURNISHED

Billhead from 1920s

Willie, had taken over the running of the painter's business. In 1933 Annie employed a young assistant, Betty Rutherford (Gilford), to help in the shop. Betty started work the day after her 14th birthday - no time or money for parties in those days. Starting at 8.00am, Betty worked a 5½ day week for about 5 shillings. Single fags cost 2d although a whole packet of cheap cigarettes could be bought for 11½d and matches for ½d - a shilling in total. The shop also sold black pipe tobacco, which came in a coil about 10 – 12 inches in diameter. This was cut to the length specified by the customer, then weighed. Clay pipes cost about 2d. Orders were still taken for the painter's business with customers also coming in to collect and pay their accounts. Walking sticks were also available and hung by the front door. The business was also agent for James Hunter, the coal merchant, taking orders and payments for Mr Hunter.

Having to spend ever more time caring for her father, Annie eventually sold the business in 1939 to James Hunter.

Contributions by Frances Laing & Betty Gilford née Rutherford 2008

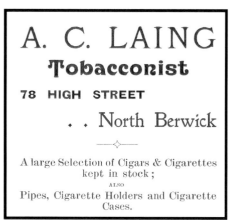

A. C. LAING
Tobacconist
78 HIGH STREET
. . North Berwick
——◇——
A large Selection of Cigars & Cigarettes
kept in stock;
ALSO
Pipes, Cigarette Holders and Cigarette Cases.

Advert from c1920

George Fowler, Motor Hirer
Market Place

Motor and Posting Establishment.

MARKET PLACE,
NORTH BERWICK.

GEORGE FOWLER, Junr.,
PROPRIETOR

West End Garage

MAY TERRACE - - - NORTH BERWICK

First-Class Car for Hire

All Facilities for Motorists

Telephone 4

GEO. FOWLER, Proprietor

George Fowler started hiring motor vehicles from Market Place in the early 1900s and soon afterwards expanded into 64 High Street and by the 1920s May Terrace. Before the Great War, he had the sole agency for Argyll cars in the area. Petrol, lubricants and Clincher-Michelin tyres were also for sale to a growing motor market. For the prosperous summer visitor, he provided char-a-bancs for hire, enabling the tourist to visit Tantallon Castle, Dirleton and Binning Wood.

Above left : Advert from c1910
Above right : Advert from c 1922
Below : George Fowler's Char-a-banc at 64 High St.

For North Berwick Ladies.

During Next week, at our Drapery Department, Market Place, North Berwick, we are making a
Special Display
of MILLINERY, BLOUSES, JUMPERS and GENERAL LADIES WEAR; also
something interesting in CHILDREN'S SHOES, KNITTED WEAR, and SOX.
Only the Latest Designs and Styles are shown, and the prices are sure to attract you.
LADIES SHORT FELTS in TAN, FAWN, SAND, BLACK, and GREY, 6/6 to 9/11.
SEMI TRIMMED HATS in BLACK and COLOURS. Chic Styles, 7/11 to 22/6.
CREPE DE CHENE and SILK KNIT JUMPERS and Blouses, varied Styles and Colours 9/3 to35/-

NORTH BERWICK BRANCH
Haddington Co-operative Socy., Ltd.

Advert from Haddingtonshire Courier 15 May 1925 (sic)

Haddington Co-op
Market Place

The North Berwick branch of the Haddington Co-operative Society Ltd opened in March 1925 in premises formerly occupied by Messrs Fowler. The property provided for tea-rooms upstairs while drapery, boot, grocery and bakery departments were all on the ground floor. Mr Sinclair from Lesmahago was the manager and he stayed in digs in St Andrew Street.

Marble counters and shelves were provided for meat and butter, while cakes and pastries were kept in glass cabinets. Also upstairs on the north side, was the bakery, fitted with the latest steam-heated oven, supplemented by a large, gas-heated plate with the rolling and mixing machines operated by an electric motor. The pies, cakes, doughnuts and scones were all made on site in the bake house, with the bread delivered, daily, from Tranent.

Born in 1914 at 15 Balfour Street, Mary MacLaren started work at the Co-op aged 14½ working as a bakery counter assistant, along side Nellie Dooner, on a weekly wage of about 12/6d. She worked from 8.00am – 12.40pm and 2.00pm – 5.30pm (6.00pm on a Saturday) with a half day on a Thursday.

Each member of the Co-op had their own unique number to record their payments and dividend contributions. When paying, a customer would give the counter assistant their store number and payment which the assistant would put into a canister along with two slips she had filled in. The assistant would send the canister to the cashier by way of a lever-operated wire pulley hanging from the ceiling. Once recorded in the ledger, for 'divi' purposes, the change and one slip were returned to the customer by the same means. This was seen as a great advantage, since the shop assistant did not have to leave the counter.

On 'Divi' days (one day in May and another in November) the manager from Haddington and an assistant would come to North Berwick with the dividend money and take up position in the tearoom, which was only open in the summer. Here the customers could collect their 'divi'. The dividend days were really busy with people coming into the store to collect their money and spend some of it on a nice cake. Saturday afternoons were also busy when the country folk would come into the town to get their messages. During the week the country folk were well served by the numerous delivery vans that went about the country.

During the summer the Co-op would see a lot of holidaymakers, day-trippers - possibly on a Guild or Rural trip - coming in for a pie or cake or even going upstairs for high tea in the tearoom. There were also those people who had come to stay in North Berwick accommodated in 'board with attendance': so-called when a landlady let a room or rooms in her house and for an extra fee the landlady would prepare guest meals with food that the guest provided. Mary's mother let rooms 'with attendance' during the summer months to earn extra money. Of course this meant extra bed linen was needed and her mother often bought her linen from the 'packwife' who came around the town in a horse and cart driven by her husband. They came from the Borders and would come round the houses selling linen, stockings, knickers and that sort of thing.

Mary worked at the Co-op for 42 years until she retired in the early 1970s.

Mary MacLaren, February 2008

Andrew Goodall, Licensed Grocer
High Street/Market Place

View eastwards in Victorian Times with Goodall's Corner in the centre left

Goodall's was an old fashioned licensed grocers on the corner of the High Street and Market Place. The properties extending from 'Goodall's Corner' down Market Place were demolished and replaced with new tenements and shops in the 1930s. The improvement was seen as being of great advantage to motor vehicles emerging from Law Road. In the 19th century the Goodall family had substantial property interests in and around Forth Street, including the Gunboat, and Market Place, from where they had traded for many generations.

Advert from c1913

Mr Hamilton was a shop worker with Goodall's. Once he was asked to deliver a bottle of vinegar to a customer in Lorne Lane. With the bottle wrapped in paper, Mr Hamilton went on his way going via Forth Street Lane. At the same time Police Inspector Watson was walking eastwards along Forth Street. On nearing the side entrance of the Auld Hoose, Inspector Watson spotted Hamilton with a 'bottle'. Suspecting a criminal act, the Inspector apprehended Hamilton and unwrapped the bottle expecting to find alcohol. He was somewhat surprised to find vinegar and from that day on, the Inspector was known locally as 'Vinegar' Watson.

Contribution by Lawrie Lumsden, April 2008

Victoria House
High Street

North Berwick Burgh Scholars c1870

The detached property at the junction of the High Street and Market Place was re-named Victoria House in 1887 during the celebrations for Queen Victoria's Golden Jubilee. This followed considerable alterations by Peter Whitecross, a local building contractor, who converted the property into a shop. The previous building had been occupied by three stances of fleshers – Struth being one of the last occupants – and on the first floor, until 1876, by the Burgh School. The Burgh School moved to School Road in 1876 when it was renamed the Public School. The old property had previously been greatly improved in 1866 on the appointment of Mr Calder, the new schoolmaster.

From the late 1880s until late in the twentieth century the shop was occupied by various drapers: firstly, James Glass who was then followed by John Grieve Jnr. They were followed by the partnership of Smellie and Brown, two gentlemen from Hamilton. Rent for the property, which was owned by the Town Council, was £60 per annum, an amount which had been negotiated with the council, prior to the firm carrying out considerable internal alterations. The partners, Robert Smellie and William Brown held an extensive range of draper products with dressmaking of the very highest order and all at economical charges.

After the death of William Brown in July 1897, William Smellie continued to trade until 1903 when the property was taken over by Hugh McDonald who occupied the property for about three years. He was followed by the Ayrshire firm of D Houston & Sons. Then in 1908, John Campbell took over the tenancy trading from Victoria House until 1925.

SMELLIE & BROWN, North Berwick

Offer this week Very Special and Important LOTS. For Instance

At the Glove Counter, Ladies KID and FABRIC GLOCES, in every conceivable make. Very Special lot of 50 dozen LADIES' TAN, CALF, KID GLOVES, sewn with all manner of COLOURS to match the NEW SUMMER DRESSES-our price, 1s 11½d per pair, sold by other Drapers at 2s 6d.

FABRIC GLOVES, New Shades and New Manufacture, at 6½d, 9½d, and 1s per pair.

Note particularly, we stock Fabric and Kid Gloves from midgets right up to full size.

Ladies' Beautiful BELTS in SILK, KID, and SEQUINE, splendidly fitted with Novelty Buckels and Clasps, at 6½d, 10½d, and 1s.

Entirely New Shapes in Ladies' COLLARS, COLLARETTES, RUFFLES, &c., &c.

Novelties in Neatly-Trimmed and Embroidered CAMBRIC COLLARETTES, 7½d, 11½d, and 1s 6d.

The New "Stock" COLLAR from 6d. Ditto, with TIE and COLLAR, 1s and 1s 6d.

Misses and Boys' AMERICAN COLLARS, in many pretty Styles, from 6½d to 1s 6d.

New Feather RUFFLES or COLLARETTES, now in much demand, 1s, 2s 6d, and 4s 6d each.

BLOUSES, BLOUSES, BLOUSES. This department is overflowing with the pick of the leading London Styles in Silk and Cotton.

COTTON BLOUSES, with or without detachable Collar and Cuff, 2s 6d, 3s 6d, 3s 11d, to 6s6d.

SILK BLOUSES, with and without detachable Collar and Cuff, in lovely New Shot Silks, also Black, at 7s 11d, 9s 11d, 11s 9d, to 25s.

MILLINERY, MILLINERY, MILLINERY.
Best up-to-date display out of the city. All the latest Novelties now added

A huge variety of Ladies and Misses SAILOR and BOAT HATS from 9½d to 5s 6d each.

Special inviting show of Ladies' Tastefully Trimmed HATS and BONNETS. New Shapes, New Trimmings, New Ideas, Popular Prices, Particularly Choice.
Assortment of Infants' and Childrens' HATS and BONNETS.

Great Variety in New Season's MANTLES. Splendid Styles, Best Value.

Ladies CAPES all the Best Shapes, and Popular Styles, from 9s 11d to 80s. The New "Bildero" Shape in the very latest production in Silk, Plush, and Velvet is very becoming and suitable wedding garment, from 21s to 65s.

Ladies' Best London Tailor Made Costumes Stylish and Perfect Fitting 14s 11d, 21s, 25s, and 30s.

JACKETS in Black and Colours.

Our special Tailor-Made Garments, highly recognised for Fit and FINISH at extremely low prices.

Costume Shirts in Black and Colours, 3s 11d, to 9s 11d.
Ladies' DIVIDED SKIRTS, in Tweed, Black and Coloured Shot Lusters, Serges and Cotton Drill, from 2s 11d to 8s 11d.

DRESSES,DRESSES,DRESSES. – A Brilliant and Huge Assortment of the Choicest SUMMER DRESSES to be seen anywhere.

LUSTERS in all Colours, Plain and Shot Effects : also in Black, 1s 11d, 2s 6d, and 2s 11d a yard.

CREPONS, 1897 Designs, at 2s 11d, 3s 6d, 50 5s 6d.

CORKSCREW, CANVAS, and COVERT CLOTH SUITINGS, 1s 11½d, 2s 6d, 2s 11d, and 3s 6d a yard.

HABIT CLOTHS in the leading Colours, including the Queen's "Selected" Jubilee Commemoration Colour, 1s 11½d to 3s 11d a yard.

SILKS.- In Surah, Bengalene, Shot, Merves, and many other makes, for Blouses and Trimmings, from 2s to 6s 6d per yard.

DRESSMAKING OF THE VERY HIGHEST ORDER. ECONOMICAL CHARGES

VICTORIA HOUSE, NORTH BERWICK

Advert from Haddingtonshire Courier 1896 (sic)

46

Following the one-year tenancy of John Smith the lease was taken over by George Annand in 1926. Previously George Annand had been in partnership with the drapery wholesaler of Smith and Annand. The firm had employed about 20 travellers who covered a large part of the country selling drapery goods from horse and hand-driven carts. In the days between the wars, it was not unusual for travellers to come down to North Berwick by train with their cart in the goods carriage. On alighting from the train, they would collect their handcart and make their way down town to sell their wares. The cart was like a mini-emporium laden with all sorts of samples. A drapery traveller would show Mr Annand samples of dresses, hats, blouses, suits, shirts, jerseys and more. Each one hung carefully ready to display to a receptive draper. People such as Dolly Sutherland and Miss Campbell staffed the shop. There was a counter on either side as you went in the front door. The millinery department was upstairs.

The business was taken over just after the Second World War by a relative of George Annand - Esther Stewart and her husband Ross Stewart. Gradually over the first year or so the stock was altered to cater for a changing demand. After the war people wanted a change from the sombre grey clothes they were used to. They wanted something new, something different and they wanted to choose their own clothes! The Stewarts introduced 'bespoke tailoring' for men and women. Customers would come in and choose a fabric and pattern and would then be measured. The order was sent down to Yorkshire where the suit was made. If someone needed a garment urgently his or her specifications could be wired to the tailor in order to speed up the process. As well as the Yorkshire tailors, stock was mainly supplied from the big warehouses in Glasgow. Some household goods like rugs and runners were also included in the new stock.

In addition to the Stewarts, the shop was staffed with three or four young local ladies. After the war the car gradually became the mode of transport for the salesman, selling his wares from suitcases. Orders were delivered to North Berwick by train, and then taken down to the shop by porters such as Jim Wightman. The window displays, including the windows looking on to Market Place, were regularly changed to promote the fashion of the season.

Eventually Ross Stewart put a van on the road in which he used to drive round the county selling. In those days business from the van was brisk, as there were fewer cars and it was difficult for people to get in from the country. The farms employed large numbers of workers who mostly lived in 'tied' housing. They were pleased to see the drapery van to buy socks, knitting wool, shirts, semmits and long johns. Long johns when displayed in the front window of the shop always caused a laugh across the road in Struths. Maybe it was the washed-out pink colour or perhaps the buttoned flap at the back?

In those post-war years the 'utility mark-up' was still imposed by the government to control prices. Each product was given its own mark-up; the amount of allowed gross profit. Shops were regularly inspected by government officials to ensure all was well. Each garment was marked with its retail price and cost price. However the cost price was always disguised in the proprietor's own code to prevent the customer knowing the true figure.

Contributions by Ross and Esther Stewart
March 2008

William Struth & Sons
59 High Street

Original Flesher's shop on Market Place c1885

The Struth family first came to North Berwick in 1876. William Struth hailed from Linlithgow and his cousin Peter Forgie from Edinburgh. Unfortunately Peter Forgie did not take to the country life and soon returned to Edinburgh. The Struths had traded in Linlithgow as butchers for several years and when my grandfather William came to North Berwick it was only natural for him to open a butcher's shop, taking over from Purves the Butcher. Our first shop was on the junction of the High Street and Market Place, at what is now called Victoria House, and near to the slaughter house which was then located where the Hope Rooms are today. The shop was the same size as the current proprietor's shop but without the picture windows, and entry was on the east side, which was open to the elements. Later on, possibly in the late 1880s the business moved across the street to the more preferable south side into what was then 1 Westgate on the corner of Law Road, trading for a short period under the name of M B Struth, William's second wife. From 1894 the shop was renumbered 55 High Street and later still, 59 High Street.

When I was a boy, before the Second War, my father ran the business. In addition to breeding and rearing our own cattle we bought at the local livestock markets in East Linton and Haddington. Normally we would buy stock for killing from our preferred farms: Whitelaw, Drylawhill, Redside, Balgone Mains and Highfield. We only bought bullocks never cows. Cows, once they had passed their milking best, were possibly sold to the cities. Here, in East Lothian, the butchers only sold quality beef. Any stock (bullocks and sheep) bought would be walked back to North Berwick and then, in the summer, kept in a field, possibly rented from a local farmer, for a week or two to 'rest'. During that time they would graze and be fed oilcake prior to slaughter. In winter, roughly from November to March, when it was too cold for the stock to be outside, the animals were kept at the slaughterhouse in layerage for which dues were paid to the Town Council. We would feed the beasts but the Council cleaned them out as it claimed the muck.

Slaughterhouse workers early 1900s
Back : Tosh Whitelaw with pole to fell animals. Back Row: Johnny Mark, Eck(Alec) Dickson, ? , Sandy Blaikie, Dod Melrose, ? , George Combe & Sam Prentice with pole.
Front Row: Jock Bell, ? , Alec Leitch, ? , Jimmy Muirhead, ? .

Although the slaughterhouse, which had been relocated up at Lochbridge in the 1890s, was owned by the Town Council they only employed a caretaker in those pre-war days. The slaughter-men were actually employed by the butchers and they worked in the shop as well as carrying out their duties up at the slaughterhouse on Glenburn Road, where Somerfields are now. 'Tosh' Whitelaw worked for my dad at the slaughterhouse and in the shop and Sandy Blaikie did the same work for Eeles. The carcases were brought down to the shop on the back of Adam Young's lorry for butchering. The cattle were quartered and the sheep and pigs brought down whole.

Pigs were bought from farm servants like the ploughman for example. Each farm worker would keep a pig or two in a crave at the bottom of the garden. When the pig was ready for slaughter, the farm worker would approach the likes of my father to see if he was interested in buying. When a deal was done 'Tosh' would go up to the

BURGH OF NORTH BERWICK

POLICE MANURE FOR SALE

FOR SALE, for ONE YEAR, from Martinmas 1900, the POLICE MANURE including the SLAUGH-TERHOUSE BLOOD and OFFAL. STRAW for the COMMISSIONERS' HORSES and the SLAUGHTER-HOUSE to be PROVIDED FREE by TENANT.

ARRANGEMENTS can be made for DELIVERING the MANURE at DIRLETON, DREM, or EAST FOR-TUNE.

OFFERS, stating rate per Ton, where sent by Rail, to be lodged on or before 24th current with

A.D. WALLACE
Clerk to the COMMISSIONERS
North Berwick, 13th September 1900

Advert from Haddingtonshire Courier 14 September 1900

cottage and kill and bleed the pig prior to carrying it back to the slaughterhouse. Here the animal would be dropped in a tub of hot water to loosen the bristles, then scraped to take off the worst of them and finally shaved prior to the butchering. The pig was sold as joints, chops, and bacon that we made ourselves using saltpeter and brown sugar.

Chickens came from the local farms, possibly a dozen or so at a time. They were killed and plucked in a shed at the back of the shop about a week before they were sold, allowing time to hang. Turkeys for Christmas came from the hill farms up Gifford way or sometimes from the Borders. Turkeys, which were not as popular then as they are now, were plucked two weeks before selling, and were featured in the shop window as a magnificent display. Other fowl such as geese, ducks and chickens were more common at Christmas.

FORGIE & STRUTH,
BUTCHERS AND POULTERERS.

REGULAR SUPPLIES OF BEEF, MUTTON, LAMB, AND VEAL.

Also, CORNED BEEF AND PICKLED TONGUES.

All at the lowest Market prices.

To meet the requirements of an increasing Family Trade, we have Opened that Large and Commodious Shop,

No. 1 WESTGATE, NORTH BERWICK.

Advert from Haddingtonshire Courier 1893

The shop floor was covered in fresh sawdust every morning to catch any spillage. This was brushed up twice a day at dinner time and again at the end of the day. At dinnertime it was riddled out the back, with the lumps disposed of and the remainder reused. The sawdust was delivered by a merchant from Leith who went round butchers, fishmongers and pubs. When my father ran the business before the second war, there were no fridges and freezers so butchers depended on a regular delivery of ice in large green lorries owned by the Leith Ice and Crystal Company.

In the back shop the black pudding, salted rounds, pickled tongue and potted heid was made. Everyone took their turn at making them, as it was part of the training as a butcher.

During the 'Season', which lasted from May through September, our shop, like all the shops in North Berwick, would see a huge increase in trade. Our turnover would more than double. The 'west end' properties would come back to life having been in hibernation over the winter, apart from any upgrading carried out for the proprietor under the watchful eye of the resident caretaker. A large number of the houses had as many as four or five staff so there were a lot of mouths to feed and we would receive two orders, one for the dining room and one for the servants' hall. I worked as a message laddie for my dad before the War and delivered to most of the big houses, always delivering to the back door and always addressing the cook as 'Mrs-' and the butler as 'Mr-'. Since there were no fridges in those days I would go into the cold larder and get an ashet. Cook would tell me the order in which she intended to use the meat and I would unload my basket and arrange it on the ashet accordingly. I never got any tips but sometimes got a cup of tea on a cold day.

After the War things were different, the gentry stopped coming and a large number of the big houses were turned into flats, many by a builder called Shackleton. The government controlled the slaughterhouse up to the end of rationing using 'allocators'. They would issue meat based on the butcher's demand, which was based on his ration voucher receipts from previous months. Delivery to the slaughterhouse was controlled by the Office of Food.

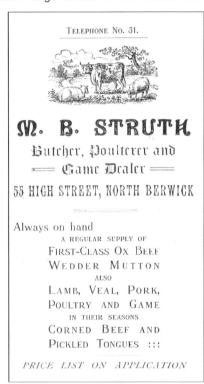

TELEPHONE No. 31.

M. B. STRUTH

Butcher, Poulterer and
==== Game Dealer ====

55 HIGH STREET, NORTH BERWICK

Always on hand
A REGULAR SUPPLY OF
FIRST-CLASS OX BEEF
WEDDER MUTTON
ALSO
LAMB, VEAL, PORK,
POULTRY AND GAME
IN THEIR SEASONS
CORNED BEEF AND
PICKLED TONGUES :::

PRICE LIST ON APPLICATION

Advert from c1900

After the war things were easier, at least from our employees' point of view because hours of work were not as long. Before the war we started at 6.00am and were expected to work until 6.00pm weekdays and 8.00pm Saturdays. During the season it could be a lot longer if orders from the west end came in late. After the war, hours soon came down to 48 hours per week.

My son, Ian, took over the running of the business in 1986 and continued operating the butcher's shop until September 2000.

Sandy Struth,
April 2008

Robert Bee, Joiner, Auctioneer and Valuer
69 High Street

Above : David Bee, Arthur Ford, Morag Bee, Stanley Ford, Jack Buchanan c1950

Robert Bee established his business at St Andrew Street, purchasing a house, shop, workshop and yard in the early 1900s. At the end of the Great War he bought the property at 69 High Street, which backed on to his St Andrew Street premises. His business included all aspects of joinery work and included the hiring of furniture and beach huts. His extensive property allowed him to store customers' furniture while their house was repaired or extended. By the end of the 1920s Robert was carrying out regular auctions from his salerooms on St Andrew Street with the help of his son David. Robert's daughter Morag, always referred to as 'Miss Bee', ran the office.

David went on to take over the firm after his father's retirement. David was easily recognised as he travelled round North Berwick to his various jobs, not on a van but on a bike, frequently weaving along with his ladder over his shoulder. People would delight in shouting 'Hello Davie!' to make him turn round with the ladder, causing the ladder to turn and Davie to wobble! On one occasion, when Davie and his family lived in Balfour Street they found themselves locked out. Davie went and fetched the ladder so that he could climb in the window. In the meantime the key was found, but when Davie returned he decided that having gone to the trouble, he would climb in the window anyway.

Robert Bee,
JOINER, CABINETMAKER, UPHOLSTERER, AND UNDERTAKER,

St. Andrew St. (East), No. Berwick.

Large Stock of Furniture, Bedsteads, &c., for Hire.
Bathing Boxes on Hire. *Furniture Stored.* *Antiques.*
Telephone No. 162.

Above : Advert from 1913   Below : Billhead from 1920s

TELEPHONE No. 112.

69 HIGH STREET,
And at 8, 10, 12, 14 ST ANDREW STREET,

North Berwick. ————— *19*

INVENTORIES TAKEN   **To ROBERT BEE,**   PICTURES FRAMED
JOINER, CABINETMAKER, UPHOLSTERER AND UNDERTAKER.

HOUSE CARPENTRY IN ALL ITS BRANCHES.   *ANTIQUES.*   *NEW & SECOND-HAND FURNITURE WAREHOUSE.*   *FURNITURE STORED.*

AUCTIONEER & VALUATOR.   LOCAL AGENT FOR MINIMAX FIRE EXTINGUISHER.

His regular monthly auctions were something to behold and were well worth attending. Perhaps a trifle eccentric, he could mesmerise the audience with his entertaining behaviour and captivating performance which was talked about for days after the sale. His quips about local folk were always taken in good part, for example, "The red wine stain on this excellent carpet was the result of Mrs -'s over indulgence." Davie loved going to the Picture House. Comedies were his favourites but usually he was slow to get the joke, so his loud laugh would ring out later. The rest of the audience got double value – the joke itself and then Davie's infectious laugh.

ROBERT BEE,
CABINETMAKER and UPHOLSTERER,
AUCTIONEER and VALUER,
69 HIGH STREET, NORTH BERWICK.

AUCTION SALES of all kinds Conducted Within his SALEROOMS, 8 ST. ANDREW STREET, or elsewhere as desired.
Inventories and Valuations made up for all Purposes.
Moderate Terms.   Prompt Settlement.

Advert from 1920

When Davie retired he and Mrs Bee moved to Duns, and North Berwick lost one of its great characters. The property was sold to Woolworths, in 1953.

Contribution by Jean McEwan
March 2009

53

John Robertson & Son, Fruiterer
71 High Street

High Street looking west in 1911 with Robertson's fruit shop on the extreme left, and George Sim's drapers shop on the right. The Temperance Hotel can be seen in the centre with the crow-stepped gable and turret of the Forester's Hall in the distance.

Betty Turnbull came to North Berwick in 1947 aged 20 when her father got the job as assistant gardener at Marley Knowe working for Mrs Esmond. They came from Wauchope, Bonchester Bridge near Hawick. Betty was still working for the Forestry Commission, with whom she had worked since leaving school in the borders, when her mother let her know that she had found her a job in North Berwick with Robertson's, the fruiterers. Her mother had noticed an ad in Robertson's window for a shop assistant. Mrs Turnbull made enquires on behalf of her daughter with Miss Bell, the manageress and sister-in-law to the owner, Mr Robertson. Miss Bell lived in the flat above the shop with her mother. Betty got the job without being seen and was told to start the following Monday at 8.30am sharp! Hours of work were to be 8.30am – 5.30pm with one hour for lunch and a half-day on a Thursday with pay to be 10 shillings per week.

In reality, Betty's hours were somewhat different. Many a night she was expected to work past 5.30pm and in the summer months it was not unusual to work until 8pm or 9pm at night, delivering orders. However she did get all day Monday off during May, June and October and during the winter she got all day Thursday off.

As well as Miss Bell, Ann Yorkston used to work in the shop. Robertson's also had message boys: two in the summer and one over the winter. Some of the boys who worked as message boys were George Muir, Jackie Bisset, John Flynn and Betty's brother Sandy. Mr Robertson owned the gardens at Smiley Knowe and spent a lot of time there growing some vegetables along with his main crop of tomatoes. Most of this produce went to the market in Edinburgh and his tomatoes were very popular as he had a reputation for good quality early Scotch tomatoes. He also had land down at East Linton where he grew peas and other vegetables. In 1948 there was a bad flood and the pea crop, which was mainly to be sent to market, was badly damaged; the shells were mouldy and damp. Ann and Betty shelled the whole crop to sell in the shop.

During the summer months the days were extremely busy. They never had a minute and were never allowed a tea break. The big houses at the west end were busy with their owners or tenants and the housekeepers would come in or phone up their order. Betty remembers Mrs Sinclair, the housekeeper at Hyndford coming in regularly every Friday during the season with the weekend order. She was dressed in black from head to toe and could be quite stern. Mrs Hare, house keeper at Dunearn on

JOHN ROBERTSON & SON
Purveyors of **Choice Fruits, Flowers & Vegetables**
grown in our own Nurseries at Knowesmill
71 HIGH STREET, NORTH BERWICK

Wreaths &
Bouquets
made to order

88

Advert from 1928

West Bay Road, spoke in a posh voice and would telephone the order in, asking more often than not for 'a nice, white-faced cauliflower'. Miss Maxwell from Peterhead was house keeper at East Gribton and often bought a 'good bunch of licks (leeks)'. During the day the shop would be inundated with day-trippers from the west, particularly bus parties of Women's Guilds and Rurals, wanting to buy the early Scotch tomatoes.

Miss Bell, known affectionately as 'flower bell' was always busy with the flowers. She prepared flowers for most of the occasions in the town and for the Abbey Church. Mr Robertson bought the flowers on a Thursday after he had been to the market in Edinburgh. Cut flowers were mostly bought for the weekend. Other deliveries came from Mr Sinclair from Congleton who came into the shop every Saturday evening, to get his order and delivery instructions for the following week from Mr Robertson. Alec Smart delivered potatoes from Newmains, Dirleton. In those days fruit and vegetables were only available when in season. Bananas, which came in long wooden boxes from Fyffes, were only becoming available again after the war. Ann and Betty used to help themselves to one when they were hungry.

Even in winter it was unusual to finish on time. Often the shop was kept open after 5.30pm awaiting Miss Morag Bee who worked next door and did not finish until 5.30pm. Betty would await her entry and receive her order for that day. Seemingly, hours were even longer before Betty started. In the early years of the century when the Pierrots performed at the harbour esplanade on an evening, Miss Bell would keep the shop open hoping to sell grapes or other fruit to the passing gentry as they returned to the Marine Hotel or their summer residence.

Betty finished work at Robertson's in early 1951 to have her first child. Her final wage was 42 shillings.

Betty Inglis née Turnbull, February 2008

Alexander Mann & Sons, Ironmongers
54 High Street

Alexander Mann established his ironmongery business late in the nineteenth century trading from the front shop at 54 High Street, now the Skipton Building Society. He sold nails, screws, tacks, bolts, nuts - all sold loose or available individually. Household goods were also available. Mr Mann kept a tub of water and ladle behind the counter so that when a lady wished to purchase a kettle or other pouring vessel he would ladle in some water and demonstrate its pouring proficiency. Under his counter he had a drawer in which he kept old tools which people could go in and borrow, always returning them!

The business was eventually taken over by his sons, Andrew and James. Andrew ran the ironmongers while James ran a plumbing business from the back of the shop. If the job were large James would take his tools and parts to the customers in his handcart. If it were a small job he would carry his tools in an old bit of carpet flung over his shoulder.

The shop, businesses and properties above were taken over by Frank Imrie in the late 1950s. After about a year or so Frank sold the property interests to Jean and Berkeley Crawford retaining the plumbing concern until the 1980s when his son, Frank Jnr took over.

Alex. Mann & Sons,

FURNISHING IRONMONGERS,
PLUMBERS, GASFITTERS, . . .
ZINC WORKERS and . . . . .
SANITARY ENGINEERS, ...

54 High St., No. Berwick.

Drains Inspected and Tested.
Estimates Furnished.   All Orders promptly executed.
Telephone No. 74.

Advert from c1910

Alexander Scott, Butcher
58 High Street

Two doors along from Mann's was Scott's the butcher, one of five butchers operating in the town before the war, the others being Struths, Calders, Eeles and the Co-op. Scott originally rented the shop from George Sim in 1899, eventually buying the shop from him in 1929. Among Scott's workforce was young Dod Johnston who joined the firm at 14 and he can be see in the photograph below, standing on the left.

Left : Scott's horse and cart outside Purves Cottage, Station Road c1910

Below : Advert from 1907

TELEPHONE No. 131.

ALEX. SCOTT
Butcher and Poulterer
58 HIGH STREET
NORTH BERWICK

SALTED ROUNDS.   CORNED BEEF.
PICKLED TONGUES.

George Sim, Draper and Clothier
60 High Street

GEORGE SIM,
Draper and Clothier,
17 HIGH STREET, NORTH BERWICK,

SPECIALITIES

Ladies' Seaside Serges

Ladies' Bathing Costumes and Bathing Caps.

Ladies' Golfing Gloves etc

Begs to draw the attention of those who visit North Berwick to the DRAPERY GOODS he is displaying this Season On inspection he thinks they will find his Stock contains a Selection of Goods specially suited for their requirements in Dress.

———o———

THE PRICES CHARGED

for Making Up are very much below the First-Class City Houses while the Garments are turned out equal to them in Style, Fit, and Finish.

———o———

MILLINERY, DRESSMAKING, and TAILORING done on the Premises. A Large Staff of Workers kept so that Orders are Executed Promptly.

A Large Variety of Fancy Goods, Children's Dresses, &c.

| SPECIALITIES

Gentlemen's Homespun Suitings

Gentlemen's Knicker Hose

Gentlemen's Golfing Gloves and Golfing Jackets, etc.

Advert from 1887

George Sim purchased the draper's business of Robert Smail at 17 High Street in June 1887. Sim had learnt the ropes of the 'rag' trade by working for many of the manufacturing houses in Glasgow and had, in the seven years before his move to North Berwick, carried on in a similar business.

Later in 1894 he moved to 37 High Street and a few years later bought the development site at 58 and 60 High Street. One can only presume that Sim had some input into the style and design of the property he had built on the site, and in 1899 George Sim started trading from the new property at number 60 and at the same time moving in to live above the shop. Next door, 58, was let by Sim to Alexander Scott, the butcher.

Doris Combe started work at Sim's aged 13 in 1936; working after school delivering parcels to customers as far afield as Dirleton and sale flyers to all the households in the town, using the shop bicycle when necessary. On leaving school at 14, Doris started working full time with Sim's. Starting at 8.00am her first duty was to clean out the furnace and reset the fire. (Probably the same stove that according to a report in the Haddingtonshire Courier of 18 December 1908, was the likely cause of a fire in a store at the rear of the premises of Baillie Sim, which for a short time was rather alarming. Fortunately, prompt steps taken by some of the employees were successful in extinguishing the fire.) Then Doris was expected to wash the front step and polish the brasses along the shop windows. Mid morning, at 10.50am, Doris would walk up to Loretto, the Sim family home on Marmion Road, and collect a flask of coffee to take back to the shop for 11.00am, for John and Betty Sim. There was, of course, no

Sim's shop at 60 High Street c1900

tea break for Doris and the other staff. Starting at 8.00am and working until 7.00pm, 8.00pm on Saturday, with a half day on a Thursday and one hour for dinner, meant working hard! When it was quiet there was always dusting to be done! Old Mrs Sim, who was invariably dressed in black, kept an eye on the staff ensuring that there were no idle hands when she was in the shop. Once a year the stock was counted. All the buttons and yardage of material had to be counted and measured.

Peggy Logan started work at Sims as a counter assistant in 1944, at the age of 15 , and was paid 12s and 6d per week. George Sim and his sister Betty, ran the shop at that time, with two other members of staff, Betty Runciman and Hilda Thomson. They used to sell all sorts of drapery goods and haberdashery including sheets, lingerie, blouses, shirts, wool, material and thread. They also sold gents ready-to-wear suits, which could be altered, if necessary, by Hilda, the seamstress, in the back shop. Peggy, just like Doris before her, had to polish the brasses and brush and wash the doorway.

Advert from c1900

Useful Gifts For Christmas

Children are again beginning to dream of "Santa Clause," that wonderful visitor who takes good cheer to every home he visits. To assist this mysterious gentleman in his loving work, we are well provided with a wonderful Stock of Useful Christmas Gifts. There are few houses he dares miss, and I am sure nothing pleases him better than when bestowing some of the undernoted Goods.

FANCY ARTICLES
We have Single and Double Photo Frames, from 6d to 2/6; Needle Cases, From 6d to 2/6; Needle Cases from, 6d to 2/-; Purses from 6d to 5/-; Handbags, from 1/3 to 8/6; Companions, from 2/- to 6/-; Silver Thimbles, from 1/- to 2/6; Workbags, from 6½d to 1/1; Tea Cosies, from 2/- to 10/-; Cushions, from 1/11 to 10/-; Handkerchief Sachets from 10½d to 3/6.

FOR LADIES
Initial Cambric Handkerchiefs, 7d; Initial Silk Handkerchiefs, ½; Embroidered Dress Handkerchiefs, 1/- and 1/6; Lace Scarves, Silk Scarves, Wool Shawls, Fur Necklets, and Muffs; Gloves, all kinds; Umbrellas, in Christmas Boxes.

FOR GENTLEMEN
Cream and Fancy Coloured Silk Mufflers, Linen and Silk Handkerchiefs, Fancy Ties, all Shapes, Braces in Christmas Boxes, Fancy Sox and Knickerbocker Hose, Umbrellas.

HOUSEHOLD PRESENTS
Table Cloths and Table Napkins, Tray Cloths, Tea Cloths, Table Centres, Duchess Covers, Sideboard Cloths, Toilet Covers, Toilet Quilts, Down Quilts, Embroidered Top Sheets, Gipsy Table Covers, Felt, Chenille, and Tapestry Table Covers, etc., and a great many other Useful Articles at

GEORGE SIM'S
37 and 39 High Street
North Berwick

Sim's Christmas advert
from Haddingtonshire Courier
23 December 1898

When an item was sold the money was taken over to the office where the Sim sisters worked. Betty Sim would record the sale and count out the change, which was returned to the customer.

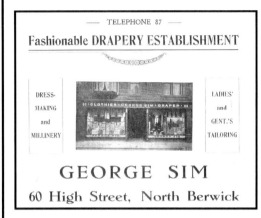

—— TELEPHONE 87 ——

Fashionable DRAPERY ESTABLISHMENT

DRESS-		LADIES'
MAKING		and
and		GENT.'S
MILLINERY		TAILORING

GEORGE SIM
60 High Street, North Berwick

Advert from 1922

During the war Peggy remembers the Polish soldiers and ATS coming in and spending their clothing coupons. Most of what they bought was sent back to Poland to clothe their family and friends. It wasn't always easy to communicate as few of them spoke good English, however they managed, even with the more discreet items of lingerie, with some sign language and pointing. When they got a delivery of Nylons, which were in scarce supply, Miss Sim would beckon her favourite regulars over to her office where they could peruse the latest delivery.

Almost every day a delivery of goods from the station would be brought down to the shop in a station lorry driven by Jim Wightman or Bert Young.

Sim's drapery business was acquired by Robert Aitken in the late 1940s.

Contributions by
Doris McAllister née Combe, October 2008
Peggy McNicoll née Logan, February 2008

Dalrymple Buildings
High Street

The Dalrymple Buildings were built by Mr Andrew Wright, a joiner from Leggate-land, Stockbridge, Edinburgh and completed in 1878. They were built on the site of John Auld's warehouse and cabinetmaker's shop that had been destroyed by fire in 1876. This is on the west of Balderstone's Wynd on what was then part of West-gate. Unfortunately, the development was not a financial success with Mr Wright facing bankruptcy as the buildings neared completion. Originally to be called Dalrymple Place, George Ferrier in his 1878 Guide to North Berwick described the property as: 'a large block of buildings – it is more like an Edinburgh block than for a small country town, consisting of nice roomy houses, commodious shops, lofts, and a large hotel, commanding for the tourist a splendid view of sea and land.'

On the 14th September of that year the buildings were put up for sale by auction by Dall & Miller, C.A., the Trustees for Mr Wright, at Dowell's sale Rooms in Edinburgh, and were described as follows :-

'That substantially built NEW TENEMENT in WESTGATE, NORTH BERWICK known as Dalrymple Buildings, consisting of three large shops and six superior dwellings all let with cellars, washhouse, boiler and back green. The buildings are all elegantly furnished, and command an extensive sea view. Total Rental £253, Feu Duty £22 10s.'

Unfortunately a buyer was not found and they were readvertised for sale on 22nd November, described as follows: -

'For Sale together or separately, to yield a high return, 3 large shops and 6 dwelling houses all newly papered and painted and having grates, gas fittings and Venetian blinds.'

The property was purchased by Ferguson & Davidson, Timber Merchants from Leith, presumably as an investment. Five years later, in September 1883, the property was again put up for sale with an upset price of £6750. Yet again the property failed to find a buyer. It was not until 14 March 1890 that the Courier announced that the Dalrymple Buildings had changed hands to Mr Stewart, late managing partner of the Edinburgh and Leith Brewery Co.

During those early years of the buildings' life, the flats had many different tenants from many varying trades and professions including a professional golfer, caddies, fishermen, harbour master, butler, shoemaker, butcher, carter, watchmaker, an agent for the Clydesdale Bank, compulsory officer, photographer, ironmonger, drill instructor, painter, druggist, flesher, joiner, tailor, stationer, spirit dealer, plasterer, baker, labourer, organist, clerk, golf club maker, blacksmith, railway porter, innkeeper, lodging-house keeper, clothier, engineer, school board officer, slater, and a postman.

NORTH BERWICK-DALRYMPLE BUILDINGS

For sale, within DOWELL'S ROOMS, George Street, Edinburgh,
on WEDNESDAY, 17th October 1883 at One o'clock Afternoon.

Those TWO SUBSTANTIAL and WELL FINISHED TENEMENTS known as DALRYMPLE BUILD-INGS, consisting of LICENSED PREMISES, SHOPS and DWELLING-HOUSES, situated in the WESTGATE of NORTH BERWICK, in one lot, at the Upset Price of £6750, Feu £45. If not Sold in One Lot, the SUBJECTS will be exposed in Two lots. *Lot First* being the WESTMOST TENEMENT, consisting of 3 Shops with Cellars, and 3 Flats above, containing 6 Dwelling-Houses; Upset, £3190 ; Feu £21 5s. *Lot Second*, being the EASTMOST TENEMENT, consisting of 3 Shops with Cellars, and 3 Flats above, containing 6 Dwelling-Houses; Upset, £3690 ; Feu £26. If not Sold in said Two Lots, the Whole Subjects will be exposed in the following Lots, viz:-

	Upset Prices	Feu Duties
Lot 1. Shop (Abbot) £500		£3 0
Lot 2. Shop (Hutchison) £500		£3 0
Lot 3. Shop (Eeles) £700		£4 0
Lot 4. 1st Flat above said shops........................... £540		£4 0
Lot 5. 2d Flat do..£500		£4 0
Lot 6. 3d Flat do £450		£3 0
Lot 7. Licensed Shop (Black) £1100		£5 5
Lot 8. Shop (Hutchison) £500		£3 10
Lot 9. Shop (Baxter) £500		£3 10
Lot 10. 1st Flat above said shops £580		£5 0
Lot 11. 2d Flat do..£530		£5 0
Lot 12. 3d Flat do..£480		£4 0

The flats above the shops were constructed in view of being occupied as a HOTEL, for which, in the steadily increasing Town of North Berwick, there is an excellent opening. If desired, Lots 4,5,6,10,11,12 will be put together. Upset £3080. Feu £25. Apply to James Sommerville, Solicitor,

Above : Advert from Haddingtonshire Courier
1883 - notice that the shops have been divided.
Bottom left : Advert from c1920 showing entrance
to hotel on the south east corner of the building.
Bottom right : Advert from 1922

James T Brodie's Dairy
72 High Street

Advert from 1913 publication

James Brodie was born at Mount Fair Farm, near Swinton in Berwickshire in 1880. He was the son of John and Agnes, and the eldest of their six children. His mother, Agnes nee Lauder, from Edinburgh, was the daughter of a wealthy tea importer, and when she married she had a dowry of £1000 along with household chattels of linen and pewter. Around 1900 James left Scotland and went to seek his fortune in the United States. He found work on a ranch in Casper Wyoming but returned to Scotland in 1906 on the death of his mother.

Later, in 1907, James took over the dairy business of John Clark. John Clark, a farmer from Wamphrey, established his dairy at 72 High Street, part of the Dalrymple Buildings, in 1887. Soon after taking over the business James advertised for a manager, and took on Mary McBain, a Huntley girl who had been living in Edinburgh. She moved down to North Berwick, living in the turret room of the Dalrymple Buildings, and ran the shop while James carried out his other duties.

Prior to leaving on his first trip to the United States, James T Brodie, rear left, with his brothers Arthur, back right, and John, front left and their cousin Fred Grant, front right. c1900

James obtained his daily delivery of milk from Wamphrey Farm, firstly from Mr Clark who also advised James on his purchase of dray horses, and then Mr Mitchell. Work started at 5.00 am in the shop basement where firstly the milk was separated into milk and cream. Later the first delivery of milk was made by James and his two men assisted by three boys. The delivery was made by horse-drawn drays, which were kept at Bell's stables in Market Place (now Semichem). The drays were kept downstairs with the horses above. A

This advert from c1911 was published with the wrong address

second delivery was made in the afternoons comprising milk for the nursery teas and cream for the gentry's dinner at night.

At the outbreak of war in 1914, James was turned down for service in the army but was deployed in munitions. Brodie's business was taken over by D A Robertson who continued trading from the shop until 1925 when the business was again taken over by Dumfries Dairy Co.

In 1917 James and Mary married and by 1921 had three children. That same year he sailed back to the United States travelling around the country for five weeks looking for a ranch to purchase. Unfortunately, the country was in the grips of a depression and he returned to Britain after a short stop with his sister and husband, George and Nessie Sayers, in Pennsylvania.

On his return, the family found rented accommodation in Aberlady where they lived until about 1930 when Catherine Sayers, wife of 'wee' Ben let them know that Springhill, the one-time home of the Arundel family, was for sale. The house, which was reputedly named by Arundel after the Clarty Burn, which ran down Law Road, was promptly purchased, and the family lived there for some thirty years or so.

Contribution by Agnes Gorrie née Brodie
July 2008

Advert from 1920

Post Office
74 High Street

*The Post Office male staff who presumably were not deemed worthy of a brooch! (See below.)
Left to Right—Boy Messenger ? O'Brien, Postman ? Hume, Postman ?, Postman Willie
Herries, Postman ? Herries, Postman ?, Boy Messenger John Robertson.*

Before opening at 74 High Street, part of the Dalrymple Buildings, the Post Office was previously situated at 9 High Street near to where it is today. The telephonic department opened at the end of the nineteenth century, at 28 High Street, above what is now the Cooperative Funeral Directors. In 1906 the Post Office moved along to new purpose built premises in the Westgate.

Extract from Haddingtonshire Courier 16 July 1897

'The Post Office, which was recently removed into commodious premises in Dalrymple Buildings, has now been fitted up to meet all requirements. The painting and decorating are very tasteful. The Postmaster's office has an exit both to the front and back offices, and the back offices contain also a retiring room for the staff, consisting of five lady clerks. The premises are light and airy, and in the front room every attention has been paid to the public convenience. As showing her appreciation of the general courtesy of the staff, it may be mentioned that a lady, who had occasion to transact a fair amount of postal business during the season, has generously presented each of the ladies of the staff with a handsome brooch as a souvenir.'

James Coventry & Son, Fishmonger
74 High Street

In June 1925 James Coventry from Milnathort, an electrician with the merchant navy, opened his fishmonger's and ice merchant's business at 74 High Street. The shop had been occupied by John McKellar, the plumber and heating engineer, from about 1907, and before that the Post Office.

Initially all the produce was bought locally, line-caught fish being his speciality. Locally caught crabs and lobsters were also on sale. James also obtained fish from Newhaven, Eyemouth and Port Seton.

JAMES COVENTRY

Telephone No. 248. Telephone No. 248.

Fishmonger and Ice Merchant

LOCAL LINE FISH A SPECIALITY

PERSONAL ATTENTION TO ALL ORDERS

74 HIGH STREET, NORTH BERWICK

Advert from 1926

Shop hours were long with some mornings the shop opening punctually at 7.30am, only after the shop window had been dressed and the shop cleaned and fresh sawdust spread on the floor. The window, of course, had a marble display, which ran with cold running water. Opening hours extended into the early evening particularly during the summer season when the west end villas were occupied.

After the war James was joined in the business by his son Frank . By this time the fish was being bought from David Nicol & Son in Aberdeen and was being delivered daily by train. Frank took over the business in 1954 after the sudden death of his father. At that time the fish was being delivered by lorry with which Frank rendezvoused at Pencraig lay-by on the A1, just outside East Linton. This happened about four times a week and it was not unknown for Frank to be waiting patiently for the lorry at midnight, with the shop still requiring to be open at 7.30am. In addition to fish, crabs and lobsters, Frank also sold eggs from John Bourhill at Fenton Barns; sausages from Palethorpes and chickens from Bob Watt at the Boggs Holdings. Later still, probably from the 1960s, Frank started getting his shellfish from Bill Dunn and Sandy Russell who had started operating out of the harbour in the town.

LOCAL FISH
a speciality
HOTELS, BOARDING HOUSES
AND VISITORS' ORDERS
PROMPTLY EXECUTED

JAMES COVENTRY
Fishmonger and Ice Merchant
Telephone 248

PERSONAL ATTENTION
GIVEN TO ALL ORDERS
96 HIGH STREET
NORTH BERWICK

Frank continued trading until 1982 when he sold on to Jimmy Chalmers, who had been with the firm since he was a message boy in the 1950s.

Contribution by Ina Coventry
August 2008

Advert from 1930s

George Shiel and Sons, Grocer and Wine Merchant
82 & 84 High Street

G Shiel & Sons' shop decorated for the Coronation of King George VI in 1937

George Shiel and Sons, grocer and wine merchant, was established in the mid nineteenth century by George Shiel. On the death of George Shiel in 1883 his wife was forced to sell the business, as at the time it was not appropriate for a *lady* to own or run a high street establishment. At the time she and her family were living in Hamilton Cottage, now the Oaks, which she continued to occupy and run as a boarding house. The grocery business was taken over by Mr Cowan although Mrs Shiel retained the property for many years.

As well as being a licensed grocer George Shiel & Son was also a House Agent acting on behalf of a large number of clients. Annually the firm published an "Up to Date Guide to North Berwick" which was made available to interested parties and prospective tenants. Included in the publication was a list of the available property in the town. The edition for 1908, which ran to over 160 pages, included 15 Hotels, 238 Houses and other properties, and a further 100 or so properties that were available 'with attendance' that is bed and board where the food is provided by the

Advert from 1898-note the Post Office was actually two doors along at 74 High Street

UP-TO-DATE GUIDE TO

NORTH BERWICK

AND LIST OF FURNISHED HOUSES
AND APARTMENTS TO LET

Town and Law from Point Garry

PUBLISHED BY

Tea & Wine
Merchants

GEO. SHIEL & SONS

Italian
Warehousemen

==== HOUSE AGENTS ====

NORTH BERWICK

Cover of George Shiel's "Up-to-Date Guide to North Berwick" c1930

tenant and cooked by the landlady. The houses for let ranged from the elegant and commodious villas in the west end of the burgh, which cost in the region of £100 per month, to the smaller flats more centrally positioned on the High Street and Balfour Street costing £5 per month. Properties such as Shipka Lodge with 11 bedrooms, 3 public rooms, a servants hall, kitchen pantry, scullery, laundry, cycle house and 2 bathrooms with a large garden, croquet lawn, bathing box and views over the links and sea and others of its ilk would command a rent in excess of £100 per month. The accommodation would naturally include provision for servants and of course have hot and cold water. Other accommodation that was available in the town came with its own stables with grooms' room or coach house, wine cellars, and conservatories. At the other end of the market the letting would only provide perhaps two bedrooms and a kitchen/ livingroom and use of a wash-house. During the season local papers like the Haddingtonshire Advertiser would publish weekly lists of visitors to the town and where they were residing.

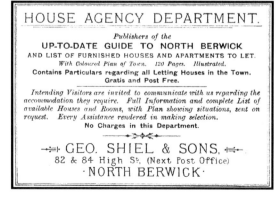

HOUSE AGENCY DEPARTMENT.

Publishers of the

UP-TO-DATE GUIDE TO NORTH BERWICK
AND LIST OF FURNISHED HOUSES AND APARTMENTS TO LET.

With Coloured Plan of Town. 120 Pages. Illustrated.

Contains Particulars regarding all Letting Houses in the Town.
Gratis and Post Free.

Intending Visitors are invited to communicate with us regarding the accommodation they require. Full Information and complete List of available Houses and Rooms, with Plan showing situations, sent on request. Every Assistance rendered in making selection.

No Charges in this Department.

GEO. SHIEL & SONS,
82 & 84 High St, (Next Post Office)
·NORTH BERWICK·

Advert from Shiel's Guide to North Berwick c1908

67

Bass Rock Cycle & Motor Company
92 & 107 High Street

92 High Street pre-1914

The Bass Rock Cycle Company, under the management of Thomas Hunter, took over the premises at 92 High Street at the beginning of February 1899, from the N.B. Cycle Company, a firm owned by José Ormiston, Solicitor, and William Ingram, advocate. That same week the firm took a stand at the Edinburgh Cycle Show displaying all the latest improvements and novelties in cycle construction, including large gear wheels (100 tooth), Ruthspiral saddles, Kohler gears and acetylene lamps.

By 1907 the Company was selling cars as well as bicycles with the firm regularly taking a stand at the annual Scottish Motor and Cycle Show, which was held at the Waverley Market in Edinburgh. Their display of pleasure vehicles that year included a 30 h.p. Rapid seven-seater landaulette, handsomely appointed and as supplied to Queen Marguerite of Italy with Simms-Bosch high-tension magneto. Also on the stand was a 16-20 h.p. Swift with side-entrance body and a Cape cart hood.

THE BASS ROCK CYCLE CO.
(T. HUNTER, Manager)
Have pleasure in announcing that they have secured those large and commodious premises, lately occupied by the N.B. CYCLE Co., at

92 HIGH STREET,

Where they will have a selection of the following High Class Machines :-
HUMBERS, SINGERS, TRIUMPHS, ENFIELDS, CAMPIONS, TRENTS, and BASS ROCK CYCLES. Prices, from £8.
Send for Illustrated Price-List.

OUR PREMISES AT 107 HIGH STREET, will be continued as a High-Class HAIRDRESSING SALOON.
With s stock of PERFUMES, SOAPS, RAZORS, BRUSHES, and TOILET REQUISITES. Also. A large selection of LOCAL VIEWS and FANCY GOODS, suitable for presents. Latest Novelties.

92 and 107 HIGH STREET, NORTH BERWICK

Advert from Haddingtonshire Courier 10 February 1899

For the 1910 show Hunter was advertising, in the Courier, that the firm's new season cycles would be better and cheaper than ever with their new model at a special price of £4 15 shillings and 6d! The firm had also diversified into the audio market selling phonographs and all the latest cylinder and disc records, with several second-hand models available at bargain prices!

The increasing motor trade required Hunter to take on further property at Station Road and 3 Beach Road. By 1910, Hunter was agent for the following 'high-class motor cars' - Daimlers, Rapids, Napiers, Siddeleys, Humbers, Swifts, Regents, Peugeots and Belsize. Trial runs could be arranged by appointment from the garage at 3 Beach Road which had an inspection pit, platform and accommodation for 20 cars!

The business at Station Road and the High Street was taken over in 1919 by J Russell and that at Beach Road by Jack Shiel.

Prior to Hunter's business 107 High Street was the premises of Gardner & Ainslie, Chemists, formerly of 58 George Street, Edinburgh. Gardner & Ainslie also diversified, selling tobacco products along with their stimulating cough mixtures!

Tom Hunter operated out of 107 High Street as a cycle manufacturer prior to moving into premises at 92, retaining the lease on 107 until 1904, using the property as a high class hairdressing salon. The business at 107 was then taken over by Joseph Larkin, who continued to trade as a hairdresser under the name of 'The Princes' Toilet Saloons.

Top : Advert from Courier from 1897
Above : Advert from 1907

Forester's Hall and Cinema
81/83 High Street

Forester's Hall in the 1920s with cinema boards by the front entrance and Andrew Aitken's confectionery shop at No. 83 on the right.

The Forester's Hall was built by the local Court of the Foresters, Court "Pride of the Forth" (No. 5686) and formerly opened in April 1887 by Mr Haldane, member of Parliament for the county. The hall was built opposite the Dalrymple Buildings replacing several eighteenth century tenements, which were in a ruinous state. It was designed by Mr J W Hardie in the Scots Baronial style, with crow-stepped gables and turret and had a frontage of over forty feet to the Westgate. The ground floor contained two shops, one either side of the main door, with two dwelling houses on the upper floor. The hall proper was entered through double doors from the lobby and was commodious in its proportions, capable of accommodating 800 people. The total cost was £2100 with a further £340 for the site. Initially only one shop was let, to David Horsburgh the shoemaker, the other being retained by the 'Court' for its own use. Over the years the shops were let to various tenants including Methven and Simpson and William Kellas, the watchmaker.

The hall was put to great use by local clubs and societies during the early years. Many clubs, like the North Berwick Ornithological Society, would hold their annual show and annual general meetings there, and the local music and choral society held their concerts there too. Packed audiences would delight at the local leading lights of the stage performing in Gilbert and Sullivan productions. Jim Brodie regularly gave performances throughout the summer season to an audience of appreciative locals and visitors. In January 1906 the Parish Church held a children's entertainment evening, an annual event, for Sunday school scholars. After tea there was a Cinemagraphic display by Mr Scott.

Advert from the Courier 16 July 1897

Jim Brodie and his band in the Forester's Hall c1910

Early in the 20th century, Mr Thomas Scott started travelling round northern England and southern Scotland giving one night lantern shows. He drove around in his big Darrick motorcar to which he had hitched a generator, as electricity at the time was a luxury, and he had to provide his own. From slides he moved on to the early black and white movies and eventually he and his family started renting halls in the likes of Peebles, Dunbar, Penicuik and of course North Berwick. The Courier reported in 1913 that 'Scott's Cinema was attracting large audiences and that Mr Scott was well known for the excellence of his entertainments, and possessing as he did, picture theatres in many places, he was in an exceptionally favourable position for presenting the very best and most up-to-date pictures.

By about 1923 the Forester's Hall was being used full time as a cinema by Scott's Empires. In those days the Saturday matinee cost tuppence ha'penny, although during the depression of the early 1930s the price dropped to tuppence. If you were lucky you also had a ha'penny for sweets possibly a liquorice strap, a sherbet dab or lucky potato. However not every child had money to get in. Lawrie Lumsden can recall the times he and his friends did not have the entrance fee. They used to jump the wall on Forth street into Shiel the grocer's back yard and take a couple of jam jars each, walk round to the High Street and go into the shop and reclaim the deposit on the jars, 1d for each jam jar. Another way in to the Hall was up the lane on the east side. The cinema had its own power supply, a paraffin generator, and it was just possible to sneak through the pipework and into the cinema without paying. Lawrie's mother always knew what he had been up to when he went home with his jersey stinking of gas (paraffin). Tommy Scott's sister Mrs Hanson took the money for the matinee. Originally the screen was at the St Andrew Street end but was changed to the other end for some unknown reason. Later possibly at the time 'talkies' were introduced, the screen was moved back to the original end and curtains and coloured lights were installed. The films were made up of a number of reels and sometimes they were shown in the wrong sequence or sometimes the sound would work itself out of time with the film. All to the great annoyance of the audience who made their displeasure known with stamping feet and jeers!

The cinema closed in March 1936 for a period of redevelopment to make it bigger and better than before. The masonry work was carried out by local firm John Wilson & Co, and during the building work a casket containing newspapers for 1887, the Law of the Foresters, and a bottle of whisky were found in the foundations. The same were replaced in the foundations of the new building, along with newspapers and coins of the day, and a new bottle of whisky. Lady Colquhoun of Luss reopened the new cinema, complete with balcony, on July 7 1938.

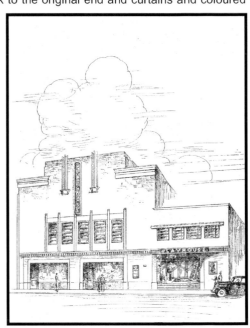

Artist Impression of the new Playhouse—taken from the first night Souvenir Brochure

The first film was a showing of 'Heidi' starring Shirley Temple. All agreed that the Playhouse was the last word in comfort and luxury. Admission prices were Stalls: ninepence and a shilling; Balcony: one and six; and Circle: two shillings. It was the heyday of cinema-going, with queues often forming outside, round the building up to St Andrew Street. Aitken's sweetie shop would stay open tempting filmgoers with his array of confectionery.

By that time Scott's Empires were now part of Inverness-based Caledonian Cinemas, which had cinemas throughout Scotland. Tommy Scott was the manager at North Berwick and was often found on duty dressed in evening suit and starched shirt. The staff including usherettes and commissionaire wore smart green and gold uniforms.

During the war, the Forces in the area made good use of the cinema and many and varied were the uniforms in the audience, including those of the forces posted from abroad. After the war the cinema continued to provide family entertainment but by the late 50s and early 60s audiences started to dwindle. Television was replacing the cinema in satisfying people's need for entertainment. Inevitably, The Playhouse closed in 1986 to be replaced by Tigh Mohr, retirement flats.

Contributions by
    Jean Crawford, Alan Hutchison, Lawrie Lumsden, Oliver McKemmie,
       Mary MacLaren, Johnanna Scott, & Ross Wilson

                    2008

The Playhouse prior to its demolition

Requiem For A Cinema

Today the picture house is coming down
And memories once a golden brown
Of Pearl White and green gate queues
Pea shooter fights and jam jar dues
Now gone..............
Today brave Caledonia's reign is o'er
No longer stands the welcome door
For Forester dance in a bygone age
And choirs and operas upon the stage
All gone.................
Today the dump truck takes away
The stones of silence in their day
And early talkies with turns between
The haunt of chummies to kiss unseen
Long gone...........

Lawrie Lumsden,
November 1986

73

James Fraser, Painter
87 High Street

Advert from 1911	*Advert from 1907*

James Fraser was born in Crieff in 1876 and came to North Berwick in 1902 as painter and paperhanger working for Grieg at 14 High Street. His wage with Grieg's was 2½ d per hour. This was ½ d more than a painter because he was a trained paperhanger. He took over the business of Alexander Allan, painter, at 87 High Street around 1912 and traded there, renting the shop from Francis Eeles, until just after the start of the Great War. In the shop he sold paint and accessories as well as etchings and postcards by the artist R Phillimore, which are much sought after today by collectors. The shop was taken over by Robert Whyte, the barber, in 1914. James moved to Forth Street trading from home, first at number 14 and then 12, as well as keeping a store, firstly at Melbourne Place and then at Abbey Road.

Contribution by Jean Crawford née Fraser, February 2008

James Fraser in the Japanese Garden at Westerdunes, then owned by Mr John Menzies, a client. c1920

Robert Whyte, Barber
87 High Street

View of High Street, looking east, about 1930 with Edington's in the foreground, the single storey shop of Robert Whyte followed by the crow stepped gable of the Forester's hall.

The pantiled shop of Robert Whyte, here at 87 High Street, was demolished along with the Forester's Hall to make way for the new Cinema building. Robert Whyte, who previously traded at 95 High Street, was a hairdresser as well a purveyor of fancy goods and toys. In the 1920s Laurie Lumsden remembers, as a young boy, frequently buying wee cobles to sail in the rock pools on the West Beach. At 6.13pm the High Street is still fairly busy suggesting it may be summer time when the town would be busy with visitors. However, most of the pedestrians are well wrapped up which would suggest that the weather was no better then than it is today.

ROBERT WHYTE
HAIRDRESSER
Stationer and Fancy Goods
95 HIGH STREET
NORTH BERWICK

Ladies' Ornamental Board Work Done
PRIVATE ROOM FOR LADIES

Large Stock of *TOILET REQUISITES*

Pictorial Post Cards, Views, and Presents to suit all
ALBUM OF 39 VIEWS, ONE SHILLING

Advert from 1910

Edington's, Grocers and Wine Merchants
89/91 High Street

Edington's c1922 with Forester's Hall in the background with Whyte, the barbers, in between.

Edington's was a very popular licensed grocer established in the nineteenth century. Latterly the business was run by two Edington sisters. They sold the best of produce in their shops in North Berwick and Gullane. Their policy was 'to sell only such merchandise as they could unreservedly recommend and guarantee, at the lowest prices known for such qualities, and to maintain a service in keeping with the character of their merchandise and patronage.' They also wished customers to know that they were 'wine shippers and wine merchants, taking a serious interest in the actual wines shipped, quite apart from the commercial side of creating sales. That having been brought into touch with some of the most important wine houses in various wine-producing centre, they naturally only shipped wine that appealed to them

Advert from 1878 at the time Edingtons moved into premises at 16 West Gate, later renamed 89/91 High Street.

as representing honest value, and offered the wine only when they themselves were satisfied that the wines had developed such character as would render it welcome to the most knowledgeable connoisseur.'

Edington's also ran a house agency department, which was under the care of Edith Brodie between the wars. Prospective clients were offered free advice on the availability of property in the burgh and its environs, which would have been extremely useful, particularly at that time, "since there was considered to be a dearth of vacant houses, owing to various operating causes, but by making known one's requirements in quarters which may be helpful, a better opportunity of securing a house is opened". Any intending resident was encouraged to "outline the nature of their requirements, stating whether a furnished or unfurnished house is desired, and whether the desire is to buy or to rent, and the extent of the accommodation required" and Messrs Edington would delight in sending, free of charge, particulars of property which conformed to the wishes of the applicant.

The business was eventually taken over by Mr Farquarson who stayed in Arnhall, Fidra Road.

The Edington family's greatest legacy to the town is the eponymous cottage hospital located on St Baldred's Road, which was funded by money bequeathed by Miss Elizabeth Edington. She had directed her trustees to pay

M. & A. EDINGTON

(Established 1823)

Family Grocers and

Wine Merchants

HIGH STREET

NORTH BERWICK

— AND —

ROSEBERY PLACE

GULLANE

House Agency Department

FULL INFORMATION ABOUT FURNISHED HOUSES AND APARTMENTS TO LET.

TELEPHONE No. 1.

Advert from c1926

to the Provost, magistrates and Town Council, the sum of £10000, free of legacy duty, in trust to erect and maintain a Convalescent Home to be called 'The Edington Convalescent Home' providing an accident ward and also a ward for sickness, non-infectious and not incurable—the latter to be kept expressly for inhabitants of the town and its environs. The home was formally opened in October 1913 by Miss Webster, a niece of Miss Edington.

John Wilson & Sons, Builder
93 High Street

John Wilson first came to North Berwick from Tranent in the late 1890s. He and his two brothers, Andrew and George, were builders to trade, operating under the name John Wilson & Sons. They purchased Fernbank, 13 School Road, which provided Andrew and his wife Jane with a home and the firm with an office, while John and George stayed in Tranent. A few years later John moved to North Berwick when the firm took over the lease on 93 High Street, from where they operated from the workshop at the rear of the property, with their cousin Jessie running the shop, trading as a house furnisher. Amongst the many jobs he carried out was the building of Dirleton Primary School in 1912. Unfortunately a bad debt in the early 1930s forced the firm into bankruptcy and so John's sons - Andrew, Willie, Harold and Johnnie - had to strike out on their own.

Johnnie Wilson set up in business on his own account and was soon gaining major contracts for local work including the building of the Cinema, the new Police Station and the extension to the Royal Hotel. Johnnie had the rights to excavate stone and aggregate from The Law quarry. At the outbreak of war Johnnie ceased trading when, the Ministry requisitioned all his vehicles and equipment. Johnnie never went back to the building business after the war, instead he stayed with the Ministry of Works for whom he had worked during the War.

Ross Wilson
October 2008

Top : Advert from 1907
Above : John Wilson's lorry decorated for a Fancy Dress parade 1920s

78

Heggie's, Joiners & China and Glass Merchants
93 High Street

The Heggie family traded from 93 High Street from about 1935 taking over the property from John Wilson. Mary ran a china, glass and fancy goods merchants in the front shop while her brothers George and Stair ran their own joinery business from the rear of the property, with a workshop and wood store entered from St Andrew Street. Their other brother, Bob, was a jobbing gardener in the town.

The joinery business was run by Stair with George working alongside, although from about 1955 they reversed roles. Previously during the depression of the thirties, each had taken himself abroad to work, with George travelling to India and Stair to Peru.

John Masterton started with Heggie's as their first apprentice joiner in 1952,

Heggie's shop at 93 High Street c1950

just before his 15th birthday when his pay was 35 shillings for a 44-hour week. George Kelly, a journeyman joiner was the only other employee. Part of an apprentice's duties was making tea and coffee when required, sweeping up the workshop on a Saturday morning, burning all the shavings in the yard and pushing the hand barrow from job to job.

It was not always necessary for the young Masterton to make the coffee particularly when they were working at the workshop or nearby. George Kelly had an arrangement with the Oak Café, where George would walk round to the café at ten o'clock with his canvas bucket, which doubled as his shopping bag, inside of which was a large brown enamelled tea pot. He was on such good terms that he could walk through to the kitchen and fill up the teapot with coffee and collect four buttered scones. All for 1/3d! Naturally, it was not long before the apprentice was shown the ropes, and soon John was going round to the 'Oak' with the canvas bucket.

Travelling from job to job was done on bicycle, with the tool bag, known as a 'bass', tied to the rack on the back. George had panniers for

George Kelly in Heggie's back yard c1950

carrying the larger tools. If a lot of materials were required for a job the hand barrow would be used. The barrow had large, cart-like wheels about a meter in diameter and even when not loaded, was very heavy. Sometimes, with a load, it would take two men to push it up Station Hill. To slow the cart down when going down hill it was necessary to run the iron-rimmed, inside wheel against the kerb. However on more than one occasion the cart went careering down the hill, once with a small piano loaded on. Fortunately when it skidded to a stop and the piano bumped to the ground, not too much damage was done - at least nothing that could not be mended back at the workshop. Sometimes George Heggie would drive men and materials to a job in his Morris.

In 1953 Heggie's were given the contract to upgrade and re-rope the flagpole on St Andrew's clock tower, in preparation for the forth-coming Coronation. The flagpole was still in its original state, built in to the roof of the tower. Since any work on the pole was going to be dangerous and any fall likely to prove fatal, the Heggie brothers decided to improve the situation by building a six-foot high tabernacle at the base of the pole. A hole was drilled through the top of the sides of the tabernacle and through the pole then a steel bolt punched through. Thus once the pole was cut at the base and the steel guy ropes released, the pole could pivot on the bolt, albeit with plenty of human assistance to ensure control was maintained. Once a new rope was threaded through runners, the pole was re-erected and held fast by the tabernacle once its four sides were secured.

Heggie's continued to trade in the town until about 1960 when both George and Stair retired.

John Masterton, November 2008

Peggy Scott's, Tobacconist
97 High Street

Mrs Scott from Clifford Road ran a tobacconist at 97 High Street with the help of one of her daughters, Peggy. She sold pipe tobacco, cigars, cigarettes and pipes – with no health warnings in those days. Across the road in Church Road was a nice little draper's run by Mrs Ferguson. When Mrs Ferguson was giving up Mrs Scott took over the shop, as she had been given notice by her landlord to vacate the High Street premises. Peggy was very keen to have baby linen so this resulted in the strange mix of both baby and tobacco goods.

Jean Crawford, February 2008

Advert from 1930   *Mrs Scott outside 97 High Street*

Peggy Logan started working with Peggy Scott in the early 1950s working full time for £3 and 10s per week and staying for about three years. Rene Melrose nee Bertram worked at the weekends. They sold baby clothes and tobacco goods. The baby goods were on the left hand side of the shop and the cigarettes, tobacco and pipes on the right hand side. Peggy remembers Dr Mallice coming in every week for his cigarettes: 100 Gold Flake.

Peggy McNicoll née Logan, February 2008

Adam Young, Carter and Contractor
99 High Street

ADAM YOUNG Luggage Porter . .

99 HIGH ST., NORTH BERWICK

Luggage Removed to and from Station. Lorries meet all Trains

Punctuality Observed. Terms Moderate.

Above: advert from c1907

Adam Young was born at Wamphrey in 1874 and from 1901 he ran a carting and contracting business from 99 High Street. He and his wife Helen and four children lived above the Golfers' Restaurant, which at that time was under the proprietorship of Martha Henderson. Adam's father, James, had been a forester and saw-miller on the estate of Sir Hew Hamilton Dalrymple and on his retirement became one of the first custodians of Tantallon Castle. One of James' small claims to fame was that he was the first man in North Berwick to own a bicycle.

James Young with his bicycle c1890

Adam on horse drawn lorry going down Church Road c1905

82

Adam started off in business collecting and delivering visitor's luggage to their summer residence. The visitors staff would arrive early, sometimes days or weeks before their employers, with the luggage, which would include not only clothes but all the table and bed linen packed into trunks, cases and kists, ready for transporting to the summer residence which was quickly done in Adam's horse-drawn lorry. Adam also 'flitted' locals and took on small contract work.

Adam's second oldest son, Robert, known as Bert, was an excellent scholar at school staying on to complete his secondary education, which was unusual in those days for lower income families. Bert gained a bursary to London University but because he was small in stature, his mother persuaded him that he would be safer staying in North Berwick working with his father.

Bert Young standing outside the Abbey Church with his new lorry c1920

Bert quickly took to the work, in his new motor lorry, especially bought for him by his parents. In addition to doing most of the 'flittings' in the town he started picking up work from the town joiners, builders and butchers. He delivered bricks and cement for the builders; timber and even new coffins for the joiners, and delivered the meat carcases, which were laid on duckboards, from the slaughterhouse down to the butcher's shop in the High Street. Sometimes carcases were delivered to East Linton and Dunbar - all laid on the back of Bert's lorry, open to the elements, and without the aid of refrigeration.

Bert also went to Binning Wood to collect logs for customers and sawdust for the butcher and fish shops. During the War, POWs were foresting the trees, and Adam would trade cigarettes with them for wooden toys for his children – 'pecking hens' and 'German sausage dogs'. When a German plane crash-landed outside North Berwick, Adam had the task of ferrying the pilot to the Police Station.

Bert continued with the contracting until 1961 when he sold the business to Peter Gillespie.

Marjory Lauder née Young, November 2008

Thomas Himsworth & Son, Joiners
103 High Street, North Berwick

My grandfather, Thomas Himsworth ran the cabinet-makers business at 103 High Street, North Berwick when I was a little girl growing up in Gullane in the early 1920s. The building and flat above had been built by his father. Tom's daughter, Auntie Birdie (Mary), sat behind the counter in the front shop taking orders and doing the bookkeeping. The shop followed through to a private office where customers could discuss the funeral arrangements of their recently departed; the type of wood for the coffin and the style of fittings. Through the back were the workshops that led on to St Andrew Street. It was here that the goods, tables, chairs, coffins etc would be made. My grandfather even received an order to make a chair for the King on his visit to The Knoll.

Grandfather told me how his father had walked around the Lodge with Sir Walter Hamilton Dalrymple to choose an oak tree from which his coffin was to be made. Once chosen it was duly felled and sawn to the required thickness and stored until required for use. Granny used to help with the lining of the coffins prior to their departure to a customer's parlour.

Advert from c1920

The business ceased in the thirties when the shop was taken over as a newsagent by Miss Green and the workshops at the back were taken over by Willie Auld.

Jean Himsworth, February 2008

Green's, Newsagent
103 High Street

In the 1930s, after school hours, all the paperboys' bikes would be propped against the kerb outside Hannah Green's newsagent shop. In those days you could park the bike in the gutter and set the pedal against the kerb and the bike would stand almost upright awaiting your return. The message bikes, including those of my father's fish shop, would be similarly parked as there were few cars in those days. Mrs Green's shop was lit in winter nights by gas lights above the counter which she lit by means of a taper, a sort of long thin candle.

John Wilson, January 2006

Bikes parked and passing by Wilson's fish shop

Edward Danks, Newsagent
103 High Street

While with his family on a visit to Edinburgh, Edward Danks called into John Menzies enquiring as to whether they knew of any businesses for sale. Having been told that Mrs Anderson, who traded with her niece as 'Green's' newsagent in North Berwick, may be willing to dispose of her business, the Danks family took the next bus down to the coastal resort. Within a matter of hours a deal had been done and the Danks family returned home to Burntisland and their butcher's business to start making preparations for their move to North Berwick. In October 1938 the Danks family took over the business and property and started trading as E Danks, Newsagent.

Danks' newsagent shop c1960 with cigarette machines at either side of shop front

The shop opened at 7.00am and stayed open until 7.00pm, unless the evening papers were late, with one hour for dinner. The papers were collected at the railway station off the 7.36am train from Waverley. This was the train on which fish were delivered too, and it was not uncommon for leakage from the fish boxes to dampen the papers. To start with, the bundles of papers were taken down to the shop on a hand-barrow but this was soon changed to allowing the paperboys to cycle down with them and within a year or so of taking over the business, Edward Danks was collecting them himself by car. Once at the shop, they were made up into rounds for the paperboys. 'The Evening News' was delivered usually at 4.00pm by bus, but sometimes was as late as 6.00pm.

The shop was a typical 'CTN' (Cigarettes, Tobacco and Newspapers) selling papers, magazines, periodicals, stationery, pens, cigarettes, tobacco, pipes, sweets and books. Boilings were weighed into little paper bags; books were wrapped in brown craft paper and tied with string; although in Danks the parcels were wrapped with tape on which E Danks was printed.

During the war cigarettes were rationed which meant that regulars before the war were rationed to ten or so per day, but people who were not regulars were restricted to five cigarettes. Steven Mitchell Prize Crop was the main supplier of cigarettes during the war with 'Players' and 'Capstan' costing 11½d and 'Gold Flake' one shilling.

Another restriction meant that returns of unsold newspapers stopped. Before the war any unsold papers and periodicals were returned to the wholesaler for a full credit and it was many years after the end of hostilities before returns were reintroduced.

The Danks became SMT parcel agents just before the war which meant that customers could have their parcels delivered to any town served by the bus company. They would bring in their parcels to Danks' shop for weighing and payment, where a sign would be put up outside the shop notifying the bus conductor that a parcel required uplifting. Any parcels delivered to the shop by the conductor were then delivered by young Tom Danks, Edward's son, to the customer on his bike. Eventually customers would come and collect their parcels from the shop themselves.

In the late 1950s and early 1960s, Tom started going to the stationery and book fairs in London. There it was possible to buy new lines of merchandise that would otherwise not be available from the regular reps for a year or more. It was also possible to buy 'bargain' books at a time before the specialist retailer of the books existed. Tom's favourite stall at the stationery fairs was that of Piatnik, the playing card specialist. There, Tom could see the latest designs in playing cards which could cost between £2 and £6 for a double pack in 1960. Tom's extensive stock of playing cards was one of the largest in Scotland and demand was strong, particularly from Bridge-playing ladies who would travel down from Edinburgh especially to purchase a new pack of Piatnik playing cards in the latest design.

Tom Danks c1988

By the early 1960s colour postcards were becoming more common with the leading distributors being Valentine's of Dundee, Dennis of Scarborough and Mill and Laing of Glasgow. Unfortunately the quality of photograph was dependent on the day the photographer came down which meant poor weather conditions: poor postcard. With that in mind Tom decided to take his own photographs and have them printed by Valentine's. With minimum runs of 5000 or 6000 of each at a time, it meant that only one was produced each season, with Tom always retaining the copyright.

As the sixties wore on Edward took more of a back seat, eventually retiring in 1970. Tom Danks continued running the business until he retired in 1991, after over 50 years' service. The interior of the shop at the end was very much like the day Edward Danks bought the shop because Tom strove to preserve it maintaining the ambience of a bygone time, still fondly remembered by many of us.

Tom Danks, April 2008

George Wilson, Fishmonger
107 High Street

After World War One, and before I was born, George Wilson, my father, was Assistant Manager in a fishmonger's and poulterer's business in Dunfermline. From there, he was promoted and transferred to a similar business in North Berwick as manager. Those businesses were owned and operated by a company called Macfisheries. The company had newly taken over the shop of John Eason in North Berwick. My father, mother and elder sister lived initially in Melbourne Place and finally above the shop in premises numbered 107 High Street, later renumbered 123.

George Wilson and Sandy Lee at the door of 107 High Street c1926

The shop had two front windows, two counters and a walk-in cubicle arranged with a desk and glass and wooden walls with a space to talk to customers. Here my mother worked on the business books as well as serving in the front shop. Later, as she grew older, probably in the early 1930s, my sister took over some of her duties. Other employees that I remember from those early days were Sandy Lee who came from Dirleton where he lived with his wife and daughter in Fidra Avenue. He was a fishmonger and accordingly helped father in the back shop where there was a large, concrete, slab 'table' mounted on brick and tiled supports. To the rear of this slab was a walk-in refrigerator which could hold some ten fish boxes plus shelving for smaller packages. The slab held chutes down which were thrown bones, skins etc which landed in buckets and later found their way into the town refuse carts or later to John Macnair's Gilsland piggery.

Another employee in those pre WW2 years was Jimmy Brown, the delivery van driver who was also a potential salesman or hawker. He was later replaced by two message boys. Over the years these numbered quite a few but of them I remember

Peter Gillespie and Andrew Reith and many were the laughs we had with them. When Sandy left the business, one Jackie Wynn who lived in Lorne Lane with his mother and brother Peter, took over as assistant to my father and this, from memory was the way of things until about 1931. At this time, I later gathered, Macfisheries, mindful of the forthcoming slump, gave my father an ultimatum—either leave with a week's notice or take over the business paying a set amount for the goodwill. He chose the latter but with the recession, business declined and times were hard. Then WW2 came along. In September 1939, Jackie was called up to the Forces and my sister enlisted as a nurse so my parents were left to run the business themselves.

Wilson's van and message bike outside 107 High Street c1930

The future did not look good but then many food items were rationed, including meat, so the public fell back on fish and trade actually took a turn for the better. By this time I had 'graduated' to become a message laddie and frequent arguments arose between Messrs Gillespie, Reith and myself over who would take which shop bicycle, since one had a small front wheel and a large basket and therefore could carry a heavier load of fish. There were something like five or six years age difference between them and me - not to mention strength - but nevertheless I always seemed to be landed with the big bike!

In addition to the refrigerator, the fish was kept fresh with ice and this is where *The iceman cometh*! Jimmy, the iceman, came from a warehouse in Leith once or twice a week with a lorry laden with large sacks of ice lumps about 1 or 2 inches in size, and also large blocks of ice around 3 feet cubed. With an ice pick the blocks would be cut to about 1 foot cubed and then carried into the refrigerator for later use.

Complementing the sale of fish, several types of game were sold and these were prepared for sale in a room at the rear of the shop premises where I was taught to pluck and clean chicken, pheasant, goose, partridge and wild goose. Woe betide me if I tore the skin of any bird in the plucking process! Of course they all had to be gutted and cleaned too. The gutting, skinning and cleaning of rabbits and hares was also one of my duties. As I remember my remuneration for a pigeon was 2d and a rabbit brought me 3d. A rabbit was therefore sufficient for me to gain admission to the Saturday matinee at the cinema with, I hasten to add, a dumb-bell lollipop and liquorice strap chasers.

Other items for sale in the shop were tinned goods, sauces, jars of pickles and the like and sometimes in front of the middle counter was a barrel of salt herring which were quite popular although I could never understand anyone eating them—they were so salty.

'Percy' Jim Pearson delivering fish to George Wilson c1930

That then was the shop, its contents and the workers but where did the fish come from? The answer is three locations. The main two suppliers were in St Monans in Fife and Eyemouth in Berwickshire. In both cases the fish sold was caught one day and up for sale the next, after short train journeys. The third supplier was, of course local, and we dealt with 'Percy' Jim Pearson so fish could be caught and on sale the same day. My father, thus, had the edge on his competitors whose suppliers in the case of James Coventry were in Aberdeen and for Johnston & Green the supplier is unknown. They used to occupy part of what is now Wilkies on Station Hill. 'Percy' was also the supplier of crabs and lobsters and my father taught me his secret recipe for the mixture of crab meat, rusks, salt and pepper which, after mixing was placed back in the crab's shell already cleaned and decorated with chopped whites and yolks of egg plus parsley.

So there we are, George Wilson - one of three fish shops in North Berwick when North Berwick had a population of less than 3000. Due to poor health, he gave up business in 1948 and for a short time the Macfisheries took over again.

John Wilson, February 2008

Footnote : Peter Gillespie, Andrew Reith and John Wilson all finished up as Signal-men in the Royal Navy albeit at different times.

89

David Horsburgh, Boot maker
117 High Street

Above : Horsburgh's shop in Quality Street (next to white shop on left) 1884.
Below : Advert from 1878

Thomas Horsburgh, who was born at Craiglaws, Aberlady on June 5 1829, was by 1861, a master Boot Maker trading from Quality Street and living at 6 Melbourne Place. He had established his business two years previously in 1859. In 1876 he was made a 'Burgess and Freeman of the Royal Burgh of North Berwick'. In the 1880s Thomas and his family were staying in property, which he owned, comprising of a shop, workshop and house, at 14,15 &16 Quality Street.

By the late 1880s Horsburgh was trading from the West Gate in their new shop under the Forester's Hall and then, after the renaming of the eastern end of the West Gate, from 95 High Street. It was from this property that Thomas' son David Alexander Horsburgh, took over the business.

David desperately wanted to go to sea as a boy, but being the eldest son he had to follow in the family boot making business. David became a Master boot maker, and often made boots for local soldiers stationed in India, having kept their measurements on file.

In about 1901 David acquired the property at 113 High Street for redevelopment. A new property was built on the site comprising two shops at 113 and 117 with two flats above. Number 113 was let to James Murray, tailor, and the first floor flat to James Young. David Horsburgh occupied the top flat and opened his new shop at 117.

Above : David and Thomas Horsburgh standing outside new shop at 117 High Street c1902.
Below : Advert from 1907

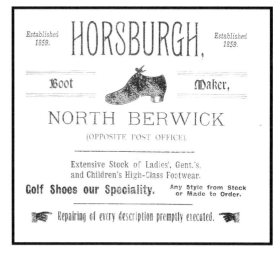

Contribution by Kathy Parker, Great-grand-daughter of Thomas Horsburgh, February 2009

Post Office
Westgate

The new Post Office just after it opened in 1907. The gentleman in the car is Mr John R Dale from Auldhame.

Building work on the new Post Office commenced in April 1906 with the demolition of the building in Cedar Grove. The new building was to be of two storeys and extend from the High Street to Beach Road. The building was opened in May 1907, and was described in the *Courier* at the time, 'as one of the architectural features of the Westgate being the most commodious and pretentious building ever used for a Post Office in the Burgh'. It was built at a cost of over £5000 and provided a front office with six telegraph desks for use by the public. There was also a telephone service from the counter to the telephone room for the passing on of trunk calls. Nine rooms in total made up the ground floor with a loading ramp at the rear and the telephone and telegraph instrument rooms upstairs.

During a commemoration dinner and dance held in the Dalrymple Hotel, in May 1907. Mr Pennington, the Post Master, spoke of the local post and how it had shown great increase in the past few years. He reminded the audience of 50 members of staff and friends, that it had not been so long ago that North Berwick was a sub-office under Drem. Mr Peter Brodie told the audience how his grandfather, the late postmaster, Provost and baker, had told him that when the Post Office was located at the east end of the High Street the indoor staff comprised one young lady, who divided her time selling 'baps' and penny stamps, always taking care to attend to the 'baps' first.

James Gray, Chemist
5 Westgate

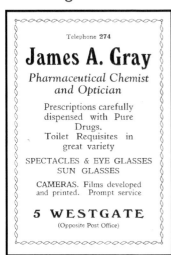

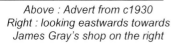

*Above : Advert from c1930
Right : looking eastwards towards
James Gray's shop on the right*

James Gray came to North Berwick in 1926, taking over the business of Gardener & Ainslie, Dispensing and Photographic Chemists, to practise as a Pharmaceutical Chemist and Optician at 5 Westgate. Before the war business was sluggish and it was a hard slog making ends meet. The shop was open each of the six working days with the half day on a Thursday while James also opened for a few hours on a Sunday, for people who needed prescriptions and couldn't bring them at any other time. There were display cabinets that provided a screen behind which Mr Gray could make pills and prepare prescriptions etc. He had a mortar and pestle and devices to make his own pills.

When the war came business picked up quite considerably as there were a good number of Polish soldiers stationed in and around North Berwick. James Gray was fortunate as he could speak to them in German and he was able to speak French to the Free French. On one occasion an English airman in the queue was listening to this polyglot exercise and when his turn came, he leaned over the counter to ask, "Excuse me, do you speak English?"

John Gray, James' son, recalls hearing of the death of George V when he and his father were invited along to a doctor's house further along the Westgate, to hear the "wireless" broadcast of the death of the King, when the 'Death March of Saul' by Handel was played.

James Gray retired to Edinburgh in 1958.

John Gray
April 2008

British Linen Bank
Westgate

The British Linen Bank opened for business in North Berwick on the 20th November 1857, after the appointment of James Dall & Son as its agent. The premises used were rented by Dall and consisted of an office and dwelling house, probably in the vicinity of the present Bank of Scotland building. Bank agents were selected on the basis of their business abilities, connections and influence in the town. Being a prominent and well-respected businessman, as well as being Chief magistrate, James Dall,

British Linen Bank c1958

was an ideal choice as agent for the British Linen Bank. As well as the bank's agency it is likely that Dall would hold a number of agencies with insurance companies, which provided a very profitable sideline. Indeed, the income derived from insurance was far more than he would have earned as agent of the bank. When an agency became vacant it was the value of the insurance portfolio, which might be taken on that was of greatest interest to potential agents. On the death of James Dall in November 1866, his son James was appointed agent. James ran the agency until his sudden and untimely death on the 23 July 1868.

Less than three weeks, later David McCulloch was appointed agent, which he retained until his resignation in March 1899. It was during his tenure that the British Linen Bank committed to building its own building in the town. The bank secured a feu from Sir Hew Dalrymple and put up a property described in the British Linen Bank's Procedure Book as a "Building of two storeys situated at corner of Westgate and Bank St and containing Bank Office and Agent's House. There is a grass plot in front of the house and office, which enter from Westgate, and a garden behind." The Bank Office comprised a telling room, an agent's room, two vaults, a book room and a lavatory. The remainder of the ground floor and the whole of the upper floor was taken up with the Agent's House. The cost was £2734 19s and 3d with £1905 7s and 9d paid to the builder and £149 18s and 1d paid to the painter. Although the property was not finished until 1872, there was a sufficient part complete to allow the bank to notify the public of the property's opening on the 25 May 1870. The

> NOTICE – NORTH BERWICK
> THE NEW OFFICE of the BRITISH LINEN COMPANY BANK here will OPEN for Business on and after Wednesday the 25th May.

Advert from the Courier 20 May 1870

property was extended in 1878 and again in 1895 to provide the property now occupied today by the Bank of Scotland.

Since David McCulloch's reign the British Linen Bank was represented in North Berwick by four further agents W.H. Montgomery (1899 – 1937), D.J. Ritch (1937 – 1957), Robert Gordon Brown (1957 – 1971), and Ivor Whytock, who took over in 1971 and oversaw the transition of the branch after the British Linen Bank was taken over by the Bank of Scotland.

John and William Auld, Joiners
Westgate

John Auld, son of Robert Auld, an engineer and weaver in Stevenston, Ayrshire, came through to East Lothian in the late 1850s. John, a joiner to trade, married Barbara Whitecross, the daughter of Peter Whitecross, the North Berwick builder and contractor. They lived in Inveresk with their three children until about 1870 when they moved down the coast to North Berwick making a home at Scott

Barbara and John Auld c1879.
Right : Advert from c1871

JOHN AULD,

Joiner, Cabinetmaker, Upholsterer, and
Valuator,
HIGH STREET, NORTH BERWICK.

FROM the extensive Alteration and Extension of his New Premises J. AULD has now made, he has every confidence in inviting the Public to inspect his Stock and Designs.

All kinds of Upholstery, Re-Stuffing, and Covering. Furniture Cleaned, Scraped, and French Polished. Curtains Fixed up. Carpets Laid. Furniture Stored.

Inventories and Valuations made up.

Cottage in Back Street. John quickly established himself in the town as a joiner, cabinetmaker and upholsterer, trading from premises in the High Street. Keen to expand his business he took on an agency for the 'Metallic or Iron Window Blind', placing advertisements in the local press for customers. By the time of the 1871 census he was recorded as employing 10 men. In 1872, John purchased his own property in the Westgate, comprising a house, shop and workshops while at the same time renting some granaries on Back Street from Mrs Bertram. He also oversaw the family's move into the Vale House on Back Street.

The Metallic or Iron Window Blind
ECLIPSES ALL OTHER INVENTIONS

OPINIONS OF THE PRESS
"These blinds have a singularly light and elegant appearance; when drawn up they do not occupy half the space of the clumsy wooden lath Blind. The friction on the tapes and cords is much less than the ordinary wooden lath." - *Architect, Sept. 17. 1870.*
"These blinds well deserve public attention." - *Building News, May 19. 1871*

Prices and Specimen at
JOHN AULD'S
JOINER AND CABINETMAKER, AND UPHOLSTERER,
WAREHOUSE, HIGH STREET, NORTH BERWICK
AGENT FOR THE COUNTY

Advert from the Haddingtonshire Courier 1 September 1871

95

Unfortunately a fire broke out early one morning in November 1876 which destroyed the front warehouse, office, cabinet-maker's shop and wood yard belonging to John. The premises were filled with furniture and the fire spread rapidly. The workmen's tools and all Auld's business books were consumed in the fire too. The total loss was estimated at between £3000 and £4000, which was thought to be covered by the Alliance Fire and Life Company. The site was eventually purchased by Andrew Wright who developed the Dalrymple Buildings.

In 1879, following the sad death of his nineteen-year-old daughter, Catherine, John retired and put his business up for sale announcing in December 1879, the transfer of the business to George Easton. The following year John sold the contents of the family home in the Westgate and the unsold cabinetmakers' stock in trade from his business. The house and other Westgate property were put up for sale and placed in the hands of his solicitor, William Donaldson of Frederick Street. It is believed that John and his family left North Berwick for Argentina to start a new life.

George Easton soon settled in to life as a businessman in North Berwick and by 1883 he had been voted on to the Burgh Council. However his business did not prosper for long, and in January 1888 the creditors of his bankrupt estate were advised at a meeting held in the Royal Hotel that his unsecured liabilities amounted to £5000, with free assets of £2000, exclusive of the extensive feuing ground in his possession, the value of which could not be ascertained.

Meanwhile, John Auld's younger brother, William, had also travelled over from Ayrshire. In 1874 he married a Dirleton girl, Mary, the daughter William Reid a slater and glazier who lived in the Old Manse, next to the Castle Hotel. William and Mary first lived in Quality Street and then in 1875 moved to Shore Street, in both cases

William Auld's shop at the Westgate in early 1890s before the building of Mafeking House.

renting from Andrew Lockhart, the carter. Mary gave birth to a son, William Reid Auld, on the 4th of August 1876 the same year that William established his own joinery business.

By 1882 William and his family were living in the Westgate having purchased property from the Trustees of Charles Lawrie, the late smith at Brown's Place, East Linton. The property was purchased for £484, 2s 4d paid for by William Reid. Over the next few years the property was quickly developed and by 1896 comprised a workshop, store, and six houses including Silverbank House, Silverbank Cottage and Rockery Cottage. Silverbank House was a substantial house built by William Auld on the site where it is reputed that Edward II and his army camped prior to their failed battle with the Scots at Bannockburn. During excavation of the foundations a trove of silver was found, which was alleged to have been payment for Edward's army after their success at Bannockburn! William went on to build the adjoining property of Mafeking House.

William R, top right, with other midshipmen of the British Princess c1896.
Photograph taken in San Francisco Bay

Soon after leaving school, William R, rather than stay with the family firm, decided to join the merchant navy, as a midshipman with the Gibson Line. His first voyage was to be on a three-masted barque, the 'British Princess', sailing from Antwerp. William was accompanied across the North Sea, or German Sea, as it was known then, by his father. Upon enquiry in Antwerp as to the whereabouts of his ship, they were told that it was moored in the middle of the river. The ship was loaded with its cargo of dynamite bound for Valparaiso rounding Cape Horn on route! After delivering its load the ship sailed to San Francisco. At this time William, like other sailors of his rank, was expected to pay for his uniform and his board while aboard. William R returned to North Berwick in the early 1900s and took his place back with the family firm, much to the relief of his mother.

Top : William Auld and staff outside Westgate shop c1910.
Bottom : Beating carpets with wooden flails on the green by Beach Road c1906.

Before building merchants were as common as they are today, William Auld would purchase his wood locally, by the tree! The tree would be delivered on a horse-drawn bogey to the yard, where it would be unloaded by winch and sawn into manageable lengths then stacked to season. Later the firm started getting their wood supplied by Park Dobson of Easter Road who delivered wood to order, all cut and

dressed. Park Dobson continued delivering to Aulds until they were taken over by Brownlies in the 1960s.

In 1907 William installed new machinery in the workshop made by Thomas Robinson of Rochdale and also a carpet beater made by Alexander Orr, Fettes Row Works, Edinburgh, who proclaimed it to be a *'World Beater'*. Prior to the carpet beater's installation, carpets and underlay were removed from houses, laid out on a lawn or green and beaten with flails. William also bought machinery of the mobile type, a Triumph motorbike, reputed to be the first in North Berwick.

William Auld on his Triumph motor bike outside Silverbank c1910

As well as looking after three or four private beach huts on the east bay, the beach huts on the west beach which were owned by Aulds, were another major part in Auld's business. In late spring, the beach above the high water line in front of the starter's box, was cleared in preparation for the huts. The huts, which had been stored over winter on the ground floor of the granary, down at the harbour, were delivered to the beach on the firm's handcart. Each of the 36 huts, freshly painted in green or yellow livery, was bedded down on a couple of bricks and would sit there happily all summer under their own weight. Invariably the huts were let to the same tenants, year after year, mostly by the season but occasionally by the month, with No. 5 retained for the Auld family's own use. The tenants would post their deck chair and windbreak requirements to the Aulds' shop in the Westgate, with Sandy Millar from Dirleton ensuring that the tenant's seasonal requirements were met. The ambience along this part of the beach with the beach huts, was of a coastal village where everyone knew their neighbours: catching up on news, preparing meals on their primus stove and awaiting fathers' return from work in the city. The early 70s saw the demise of the beach huts due to more people travelling to the Costas, vandalism and the cost of renting the beach from the Council. The huts were put up for sale at £25 each with the majority sold to previous tenants from the west coast.

In the course of erecting beach huts L : R : unknown, John Walker, Alec Miller c1933

Apart from storing beach huts, Auld's also used the top floor of the granary for storing horsehair for the uphol- stery side of the business, which was carried out by Charlie Stewart and his son Jack. The hoist on the north west side of the building was put up by the firm in the early 1900s to allow the firm access to the top floor. When the Council, in the early 1930s, placed an eviction order on the build- ing, the firm moved the beach huts, to St Andrew Street, taking over the premises of Himsworth.

Following a brief illness, William Auld died in October 1925 but his son Wil- liam R continued working in the busi- ness into his nineties, when he was still seen unloading deliveries. He was succeeded by his son William and today the family joinery tradition continues with William R's grandson, Stewart.

Stewart Auld, February 2009

Above : William R unloading Park Dobson's lorry in 1966. Aged 90!

Station Road

The Gas Works in the latter part of the nineteenth century with the gasometer in the background. Until 1860 the Gas Works were located on the West links possibly on the eighteenth fairway near the end of Point Garry Road.

Advert from Haddingtonshire Courier 23 March 1906

Station Road with the parade celebrating the Diamond Jubilee of Queen Victoria in 1897.

Following the relocation of the Gas Works to Williamston in 1904, the Burgh Council later sold off the site in two parcels, one in 1906 and the second in 1907. The sites were adjacent to another Burgh Council owned site occupied by both the Fire Engine Station and what became James Watt's shop. Both parcels of land were purchased by Mr John Campbell, proprietor of the Royal Hotel for a total of £2210. At the time the 'Haddingtonshire Courier' reported that 'Mr Campbell intended taking the restaurant business out of the Royal Hotel and transferring it to a new dining saloon of handsome dimensions' which he planned to build on the newly-acquired ground. This plan never came to pass and by the middle of the next decade the ground had been developed into a fine parade of shops. Station Road, or Hill as it is called today, looks almost the same as it did ninety years ago apart from the replacement for James Watt's shop.

North Berwick Scouts on Parade on Station Road in the 1930s.

James Watt, Golf Club Maker
1 Station Road

Jim Watt's shop with Lex Hutchison and Jim's nephew James at the door c1930

James Watt was born at Gatehouse, near Kirklandhill outside Dunbar, in 1882 and in the 1890s the family moved to Dirleton, living firstly in the Toll House and then from the turn of the century, at Rosemary Cottage. He had four brothers and one sister. In the late 1890s, James Watt's father, the head forester at Archerfield Estate heard that Willie Park Snr, a regular player at the golf links on the Estate, was looking for an apprentice for his club-making business in North Berwick. James jumped at the opportunity, and soon after started work at Park's premises on Beach Road opposite the West Links. James Watt was granted his Professional Licence for the West Links in 1905.

A little later, in 1906, Donald MacKay started trading as a club maker from 1 Station Road and continued there until at least 1909 and although James Watt was almost certainly living locally it is not known for sure if he was working for or in business with Mac-Kay. However soon after

JAMES WATT

PRACTICAL GOLF CLUB MAKER

Opposite
NEW CLUB - 1 Station Road, North Berwick

TUITION :: Copying Favourite Clubs a Speciality :: Children's Clubs

All Clubs Guaranteed Hand-Made on the Premises of the Best Selected Material—
ONE QUALITY ONLY THE BEST.

Advert from 1920

MacKay's emigration to America, James Watt was certainly trading on his own account from 1 Station Road, and continued to do so for the next 50 years only closing for the latter years of the Great War when he was called up.

Jim giving lessons to young visitors on the West Links 1930s

Jim Watt started trading again after the First War and as business slowly picked up he started employing an assistant/apprentice club maker. Among those who worked for Jim were Lex Hutchison, Alf Marr, James Wynn and Jim's nephews Alick and James R Watt. Jim used to specialise in left handed clubs – his left handed brother David won the Scottish Professional Championship in 1914. His secret in shaping left handed clubs was to use a mirror giving a right-handed reflection. It was known that Jim was an excellent instructor and throughout the summer he was to be found on the links giving lessons.

In 1938, Jim displayed a range of his hand made wares at the Empire Exhibition in Glasgow and it was following this that he was invited to give a talk on radio about golf, including, the first broadcast lesson. The Exhibition gave a great boost to the business and also benefited the apprentices when they applied for Professional posts at the end of their apprenticeship.

All James' brothers - John, Robert, Willie and David - turned Professional too, and all went on to gain positions as Pros at various golf clubs.

Alick Watt
2006

James Watt in his workshop at 1 Station Road 1930s

103

Ben Sayers, Golf Club Maker
21 & 27 Station Road

Ben Sayers Shop at 21 Station Road 1913

Ben Sayers Snr started renting the properties at 21 and 27 Station Road from John Campbell, manager of the Royal Hotel in 1912 and stayed there until 1917. Numbers 21 and 27 were used as a shop and workshop respectively. By mid 1913 Sayers was employing 10 members of staff including I. Lumsden and J. Richardson who were earning gross weekly wages of £1 2s 6d, with apprentices such as James Richardson earning 4 shillings per week, 3/8d net of contributions. From Station Road, Sayers was exporting to many parts of the globe including the United States where his son, George, was based at Merion Golf Club, Pennsylvania.

Right : Ben Sayers Snr in about 1900

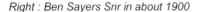

Sayers' 'Club maker's box' at Inchgarry c1910

George Sayers and Ben Sayers Jnr standing outside the shop on the West Links c1920

Sayers had previously traded from a 'club makers box' against the wall at Inchgarry, which bounded the West Links and before that at a couple of shops in the Westgate and High Street including a shop in the Dalrymple Buildings, where for a period he resided in the 1880s. When he moved to Station Road he continued to use his previous address, Ben Sayers, The Links, North Berwick on his exports.

In 1917 Ben Sayers moved to the West Links again, this time replacing the firm of James Hutchison, club maker, at the more familiar position beside the starter's box. At this time, during the First War, there were only two members of staff, including Elizabeth Sayers, wife of Ben Sayers Junior. The firm of Ben Sayers went on to occupy this position for almost 50 years.

Florence Bates, Milliner and Ladies' Outfitter
21 Station Road

Station Road 1930s

Florence Bates opened her shop at 21 Station Hill in 1920. Miss Bates, a milliner to trade, was friendly with Ben Sayers and took over the lease of the shop shortly after Sayers moved to the West Links. The shop mainly catered for the well-to-do customer from the West End. There she employed her own milliner and tailoress and nothing was ever too much effort for a client.

Mary Hutchison started working at Florence Bates in 1939 having responded to an advert in the shop window for 'Smart Girl Wanted'. Chrissie Flynn from Melbourne Place worked along side Mary as tailoress. Mary worked all her working life at 21 Station Road apart from a few years during the war when she worked as a landgirl at Highfield on Mr Simpson's farm.

One of Mary's first jobs was to cycle up the Avenue to a particular customer's house where Mary was handed a small package. This was the first of many trips to collect similar packages. The customer had a small blue songbird that she adored and so she started to collect its feathers and engaged the services of the milliner at Florence Bates to make her a hat with them!

Mary Hutchison, February 2008

FLORENCE BATES
MILLINERY :: BLOUSES
. . . LINGERIE . . .

21 STATION RD. NORTH BERWICK

Advert from c1930

George Orr, Chemist
27 Station Road

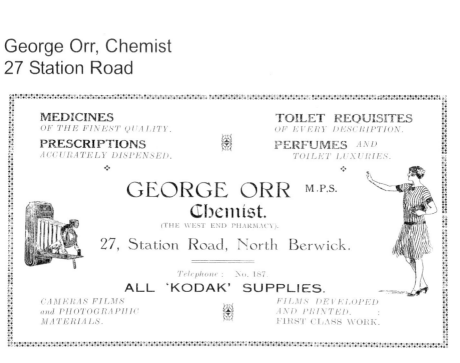

When I left school at fourteen in 1944, I got a job in Orr's the Chemists on Station Road where I worked beside June Samuel, Miss Brown the dispenser and Mr Orr. As well as selling medicines and prescribed drugs, we also sold cameras, photographic supplies and cigarettes. Most of the goods we sold were on account and that included cigarettes! As well as dusting the shelves, I also had to deliver the goods to the customer's house. It was not unknown for some customers to phone up for cigarettes and expect them to be delivered straight away, and of course paid on account. I was paid 12/6d per week - working six days, Monday to Saturday with a half day on a Thursday.

Mr Orr also owned the shop next door at 29, which was let as a hairdresser's salon called the 'Beauty House'.

Margaret Burgon, March 2008

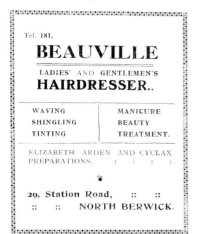

Top and Left : Adverts from 1930
Above : Advert from Courier 14 February 1930

Oliver Mckemmie, Coalmerchant
Station Road

Hugh Morton, his wife Christina and six children, three sons and three daughters, lived in Auburn Cottage on Clifford Road. Hugh a retired stonemason and his wife ran a 'hand laundry' from the outhouse at the back of their home. Christina was assisted in the laundry by her three daughters, Jean, Nan and Christina. It was their job to return the freshly cleaned and ironed laundry to the owners, and at the same time pick up the next load. Their son Dick worked for Bob Bee the joiner, while one

Abbey Church Choir outing to Loch Lomond 1910
7th from left - Maggie Ingles. 5th from right - Christina Morton

of their other sons, Bob, had his own plumbing business at 42 High Street. Their other son John was killed in the Great War. Christina, the daughter, and her great friend Maggie Ingles sang soprano and contralto in the Abbey Church choir and North Berwick Operatic Society regularly taking parts in the latest Gilbert and Sullivan production put on in the Forester's Hall.

In 1919 Christina married Oliver McKemmie in Auburn Cottage. Oliver had trained as a millwright in Dalry, Edinburgh before the War and served his country with the Royal Flying Corp. On coming down to North Berwick, Oliver soon got a position with North British Railways working in the signal box at North Berwick station. It was in the signal box that he practised his hobby, photography, taking photographs of anything that he thought was of local interest. Unfortunately his collection of half and quarter plates were lost but one or two photographs still exist. After a year or so he took up a position with Bob Bee. There he stayed until the early 1930s when he was made redundant during the depression.

Lothian Coast Express c1920 which travelled between Glasgow and North Berwick

108

Fortunately after a few weeks, he got a position as a coalman working for John Eason up at the station yard working alongside Johnny McIlroy. Eason ran a two-man, one-lorry outfit delivering coal around the town. On Eason's retiral, Oliver took the opportunity to purchase the business and when, in the mid 30s, one of his rival firms, George Hunter, (at the time run by Bob Logan) was put up or sale, Oliver purchased that firm too, and moved into their premises on Station Road, opposite the station.

Coal either came from Tranent or Fife with the best coming from Fife. The Fife coal was sold for two shillings a bag and the Tranent, for one and six. Cheaper still, was Whistlers at one shilling a bag. The coal was purchased from wholesalers like the Edinburgh firm of A & G Anderson, and was delivered by rail on a wagon. Generally the coal merchant had two or three days to unload the wagon, by hand, before demurrage was incurred, and ideally the coal merchant would try and sell directly from the wagon; bagging the coal straight off the back of the wagon.

Advert from c1935

Oliver McKemmie retired in 1950 through ill health, selling the business to A & G Anderson. Oliver was an active member of the community serving on the local Council and as a member of the Fire Brigade serving alongside his brothers-in-law at the time the burgh received its first motor driven fire engine.

Contribution by Oliver McKemmie Jnr September 2008

North Berwick's first motor driven Fire Engine c1922

John Anderson, Florist and Gardener
4 Station Road

In 1912 John Anderson took over the gardens and property at 2 and 4 Station Road after the death of the previous owner, John Dennis of Ellonville, Dalkeith, who had let the property to Mary Lyall. The property, financed with a loan of £150, consisted of a commodious villa, a four apartment cottage, seven greenhouses of 60 feet length, shop, Tea bar and Tea rooms, store, stables and extensive garden ground of about two acres lying in close proximity to

John Anderson

ℑlorist anð Garðener

The Nurseries

4 Station Road – Opposite Royal Hotel

North Berwick

Advert from 1922

the railway station. Unfortunately, John died suddenly in the mid 1920s and the business was taken over by his son Andrew.

Andrew employed gardeners in the nursery and about another 14 jobbing gardeners whom he deployed to the large houses in the West End. Jim Skeldon was his right-hand man in the nursery with the likes of George Henderson and John Lorimer working in the gardens 'up the avenue'.

In the nursery the large greenhouses were full of tomatoes and flowers. Most of the summer fruit and vegetables were sold to the local guesthouses and hotels which would buy tomatoes by the 'chip' - a tray of twelve boxes.

All the remaining produce from the gardens was sold in the shop where Ina Duncan worked. She was very artistic and made up the wreaths, starting with a metal frame, which she covered in moss, fixing it with twine. Then using the appropriate wire, as each flower had its own gauge and length of wire, she would attach the flowers and foliage. Andrew grew most his own flowers, although would import azaleas from Belgium to sell at Christmas. Margaret Burgon also worked for Andrew between 1950 and 1954, both serving in the shop and preparing the job sheets and wages.

Telephone 316

John Anderson

Florist and Gardener

GARDEN PLANNING AND ALL KINDS OF JOBBING WORK CARRIED OUT

GARDENS KEPT BY CONTRACT

Selection of Cut Flowers, Foliage and Flowering Plants. Vegetables, Tomatoes, Grapes, etc. in season. Specialist in Wreaths and Bouquets. Motor mower for hire

The Nurseries

STATION ROAD, NORTH BERWICK

Advert from 1930

When Andrew died in 1958 the business was taken over by MacFarlane of East Linton. It was run by two brothers who worked in the gardens and a sister who ran the shop.

Contributions by
Moira Dunn   August 2008
Margaret Burgon   March 2008

Gilbert's Garage
Old Abbey Road and Quality Street

Old Abbey Road garage with James Gilbert at the wheel, early 1900s

James Gilbert and his wife came to North Berwick in the late nineteenth century to take up their positions as coachman and house maid in one of the west end villas. Eventually James started up in business on his own account renting horse and traps firstly from stables next to Dalrymple Hotel. The business was eventually taken over by one of his four children, George, always known as Dod.

In 1943, Charlie Bruce aged 14, left school on the Friday and started at Dod Gilbert's Garage on the following Monday having been given the position of apprentice by the garage foreman, Jimmy Cockburn. Charlie had always wanted to be a motor mechanic. He travelled to work by bicycle returning home at dinnertime for the soup his mother had made that morning in their ground floor flat at the Redhouse, Dirleton. His pay was about 17/6d a week; barely enough, in his mother's eyes, to cover the cost of washing his overalls. He was expected to work eight till five, Monday to Friday and until 12 on Saturday. As well as the hands on experience he gained in the garage, Dod Gilbert sent him to night classes up at the new High School on Grange Road. A mechanic from Russell's Bass Rock garage named Jimmy Brown took the classes.

At sixteen, Charlie got himself a motorbike, his brother's old ex-army Royal Enfield with a pair of panniers on the back. In the days, during and just after the war, when there was not enough petrol the bike was topped up with paraffin, which caused the exhaust to glow red hot if the engine was run too long.

Quality Street Garage Decorated for Coronation of George VI in 1937

The East End Garage on Quality Street served petrol, displayed new cars for sale, and garaged cars overnight and for longer periods. Gilbert had a dealership with Morris and obtained his stock of cars and spares from Westfield Auto Cars on West-field Avenue in Edinburgh. Since space was tight a turntable had been installed to facilitate turning when the vehicles came in for parking. The turntable is now in George Milton's garden in Kingston. The garage sometimes stayed open until midnight as Gilbert's taxi rank was at Quality Street.

The Abbey Road garage stored cars as well having lock-up garages and hard standing at the rear. One of the first jobs apprentices learned, was how to move the cars around the garaging area. Since some of the cars were required almost daily there was a knack in knowing where to park the cars as they came in at night. Although not open as late as Quality Street, it was still possible to obtain petrol up until 8.00pm. Driving became second nature to the young Charlie as he was always being asked to move the cars around the garage. Some evenings Bob Millar, one of Gilbert's taxi drivers would take Charlie and the other apprentices out in an old Morris Oxford registration number WS 3651, and teach them how to drive. Bob would sit in the back and give instructions. Any mistakes were punished with a thump on the back of the neck with Bob's bunnet.

During the war the army had their own pumps in the Quality Street garage and it was not unusual to see a queue of tanks or bren-gun carriers sitting outside. Spare parts were not always easy to get hold of during and after the war so it was sometimes necessary to make a replacement part and Jimmy Cockburn was often at the lathe doing so: a big end, con rod or piston. Bodywork was carried out by Kennedys of Haddington, another business owned by George Gilbert. The damaged body part would be unbolted and if it could be repaired, sent over to Haddington for repair. Chassis damage was carried out at the Old Abbey Road premises.

After the war, visitors started returning to the town and its neighbouring villages. One of the jobs Charlie was asked to do was go out to start up customers' cars, some of which had been lying in a garage throughout the war so the brakes and other parts of the running gear were seized up. Customers frequently asked for their tyre pressure, battery water and other fluids to be checked when they came in to buy petrol and it was all part of the service that garages offered in those days. The firm owned a hearse, which was garaged down in Melbourne Mews. The undertaker firms, Aulds, Denholms or Bees would engage the services of Gilberts to supply the hearse and taxis, which doubled up as funeral cars. The taxi side of the business was very busy, with six or seven full time staff, collecting fares from the station, frequently from the London train when it stopped at Drem, and delivering them to their summer accommodation.

Willie Struth worked there in those days, before he joined Moir & Baxter, in a semi-managerial position. He always endeavoured to see that the customer was happy, ensuring that their car was ready when required and that they had the spares and equipment to do the work.

After the death of George Gilbert in the early 1960s, the business was taken over by Walter Keith Elliot a businessman from Edinburgh.

Top : Advert from 1930
Bottom : Provost George Gilbert

Charlie Bruce, April 2008

113

James Elliot, Builder
53 Old Abbey Road

James Elliot was born near Kelso where he trained as a mason, later finding work on the building of the foundations for the Forth Bridge. When work finished he emigrated to Zanesville, Ohio where he started a building business. He was soon joined by his girlfriend from the Borders and the two were married. Their first son William was born in 1894 but during the birth of their second son two years later, James' young wife died. Unable to bring up the two boys and run a business, James returned to Scotland.

In the early 1900s James and his second wife and two sons moved to North Berwick, starting up a builder's business. Soon after arriving he built 'Greymount' in St Margaret's Road for his family. When a plot of land with workshop and outbuildings at 53 Old Abbey Road came on the market, James wasted no time in securing its purchase and set to work building a new home, 'Hendersyde' on the west of the plot. Since James had a great fear of fire, all the floors in the house were cast in concrete. The outbuildings were immediately put to good use as storage and garaging for the growing building business. Among the work force were Carl Henderson,

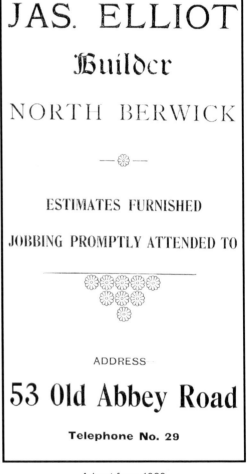

Advert from 1922

Peter Slicer and Sandy Rutherford. As well as building new houses, the firm made gravestones and demolished buildings like Gardener's shop on the corner of the High Street and Quality Street. James served as Baillie on the local council in the 1920s. When James died in 1932 the business was taken over by William who continued the firm until about 1960 when the business was sold to Andrew Thorburn.

Gordon Elliot
October 2008

George Baillie, Plasterer
Quadrant Cottage, 14 Balfour Street

George Baillie came over to North Berwick from Haddington in the early years of the twentieth century after being told by his father to 'get away down to North Berwick, there is a lot of work down there'. He started up his plastering business at 14 Balfour Street, a little pantiled cottage on the corner with Quadrant Lane. His son, William, took over the business in 1930 when George died. William employed men like 'PK' Thorburn, George Marr, Dan Douglas and Walter Miller. As well as the hand cart, William used his car and trailer, ferrying his men to jobs. He took on a yard down at the harbour next to Sandy Wilson, the joiner from Dirleton. There he kept his lime and ce-

Advert from 1920s

ment beside the scaffold batons. Most of his work came from the new estates that were being built in Gullane and Longniddry. The work comprised mainly plastering, roughcasting and pointing although he did take on ornate cornice work.

He obtained sand from the beach at Scoughall and often Carl Henderson, who had retired after working with Elliot the builder, would go along for the ride. Carl had a great interest in local history and would dig around the ground where the sand was being removed looking for artefacts, many of which he donated to the local museum. Carl would often say that one should 'aye be doin' something, even it's a load of rubbish'!

William did all his own paperwork, with everything scrupulously analysed down to the last penny so that the customer knew exactly what they had received. William retired in 1970.

Contribution by Vanda Baillie
November 2008

George Aikman, Private Family Laundry Lochbridge

L : R—Aggie Thorburn, Helen Herkes, Mrs Leckie, Teen, Mr Aikman, Annie in pram, Ben Aikman, Mrs Aikman, Mrs Ramsey Hunter, Liz McNally.

George Aikman started his laundry at Lochbridge around 1900 assisted by his family as well as employing a number of local girls. The business continued until George's death in about 1930 when it was taken over by his son Ben. At the time of his death George owned the laundry and stables as well as the family home, 'Beachview', and the neighbouring property of Glenlea. The laundry was taken over in 1934, by George Hood, who ran the laundry next door.

Above : Laundry Staff c1930
Right : Advert from 1910

G. AIKMAN'S
Private Family Laundry
LOCHBRIDGE, NORTH BERWICK.

Orders called for to any Address.

**VAN CALLS at GULLANE on MONDAYS and FRIDAYS,
EAST LINTON and DISTRICT on WEDNESDAYS.**

Having a thorough system of working,
Customers can rely on all Orders being promptly
attended to and correctly delivered.

View looking westwards towards Lochbridge Toll with toll house on the right. Aikman's laundry is centre right with name-plate visible. The other building on the left probably belonged to George Hood. The houses of 'Beachview' and 'Glenlea' have not been built and the chimneys in the distance probably belong to the slaughterhouse. c1900

A report from the 'Courier' details an unfortunate court case involving George Aikman. "SMALL DEBT COURT - The quarterly Small Debt Court was held in the Council Chambers on Wednesday, Sheriff Sherriff presiding. There were thirteen cases on the roll, in nine of which decree was given in absence of defenders. In the case of George Aikman v. Mary White, the pursuer, who was represented by Mr Wallace, claimed damages to the amount of five guineas for desertion of service without a week's notice in terms of the regulations of the laundry, where defender was employed as a marker and packer. Mr D.M. Jackson appeared for the defender, who was eighteen years of age. Proof was led, and it transpired that some time subsequent to the defender's engagement a notice was posted up at Mr Aikman's laundry to the effect that a weeks notice should be given and required. The pursuer did not draw the special attention of the defender to this regulation, but she admitted understanding its import. His lordship gave decree for thirty shillings."

Haddingtonshire Courier January 1902

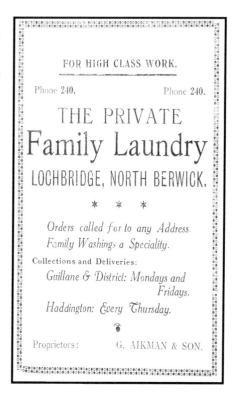

Advert from 1929

117

North Berwick Foundry

Top: View along East beach to Foundry c1890 - notice how it is built on to the beach over what is now Melbourne Road.
Right: Advert from Haddingtonshire Courier 1897.
Below: Advert from Ferrier's Guide to North Berwick 1878

Robert Bridges established a foundry at the east end of the burgh in 1828. It was located between the East Road and what is now Melbourne Road, and between the Quadrant and what is now Balfour Street. During the Foundry's lifetime of over 60 years up to twenty men were employed at any one time, receiving their wages at the porch on the side of 9 The Quadrant, the home of Robert Bridges.

The foundry property was purchased by the Meikleham family of Wemyss Place, Edinburgh about 1890 and let out for stabling, workshops and storage to the likes of John Macintyre. By 1896 the property had been taken into the ownership of the town and in 1897 put up for sale with an upset annual feu of £120 10s 6d. The property was finally sold by auction, at the third attempt, to Alexander Calder, a builder and contractor from Edinburgh.